SIMONE WEIL AS WE KNEW HER

D1553882

Simone Weil (1909–1943) was a defining figure of the 20th century; a philosopher, Christian, resistance fighter, labour activist and teacher, described by Albert Camus as 'the only great spirit of our time.' In 1941 Weil was introduced to Father Joseph-Marie Perrin, a Dominican priest whose friendship became a key influence on her life. When Weil asked Perrin for work as a field hand he sent her to Gustave Thibon, a farmer and Christian philosopher. Weil stayed with the Thibon family, working in the fields and writing the notebooks which became *Gravity and Grace* and other posthumous works.

Perrin and Thibon met Weil at a time when her spiritual life and creative genius were at their height. During the short but deep period of their acquaintance with her, they came to know her as she actually was. First published in English in 1953 and now introduced by **J. P. Little**, this unique portrait depicts Weil through the eyes of her friends, not as a strange and unaccountable genius but as an ardent and human person in search of truth and knowledge.

Joseph-Marie Perrin (1905–2002) was a Dominican priest and French Resistance worker. His books include *Mary, Mother of Christ and Christians*. **Gustave Thibon** (1903–2001), a native of the Ardèche, received the 'Grand Prix de l'Académie Française' for literature in 1964, and for philosophy in 2000.

J. P. Little, of St Patrick's University College, Dublin, is author of *Simone Weil on Colonialism* (2003) and *Simone Weil: Waiting on Truth* (1988).

Also available from Routledge:

The Need for Roots
Gravity and Grace
Oppression and Liberty
Letter to a Priest
Intimations of Christianity among the Ancient Greeks

SIMONE WEIL AS WE KNEW HER

J M Perrin and G Thibon

Translated from the French by Emma Craufurd

Introduction by J P Little

Routledge
Taylor & Francis Group

LONDON AND NEW YORK

First French edition published 1952 as *Simone Weil telle que nous l'avons connue*

First published in English in 1953 by Routledge and Kegan Paul Ltd, London

Translated from the French by Emma Craufurd

This edition published 2003 by Routledge,
2 Park Square, Milton Park, Abingdon, Oxon OX14 4RN
Simultaneously published in the USA and Canada
by Routledge
711 Third Avenue, New York, NY 10017

Routledge is an imprint of the Taylor & Francis Group, an informa business

Translation © 1953, Routledge and Kegan Paul Ltd

Introduction © 2003, J. P. Little

Typeset in Gill Sans and Goudy
by Keystroke, Jacaranda Lodge, Wolverhampton

British Library Cataloguing in Publication Data
A catalogue record for this book is available from the British Library

Library of Congress Cataloging in Publication Data
Perrin, Joseph Marie, 1905–
[Simone Weil tell que nous l'avons connue. English]
Simone Weil as we knew her/J.M. Perrin and G. Thibon;
translated from the French by Emma Craufurd; with an introduction by J.P. Little
p. cm.
ISBN 0-415-30642-6— ISBN 0-415-30643-4 (pbk.)
I. Weil, Simone, 1909–1943. I. Thibon, Gustave, 1904–. II. Title
B 2430. W474P4213 2003
194— dc21
[B]   2003043197

ISBN 0-415-30642-6 (hbk)
ISBN 0-415-30643-4 (pbk)

CONTENTS

NOTES ON THE AUTHORS

Joseph-Marie Perrin

Born in 1905 into a devoutly Catholic family in Troyes, Michel Perrin was to take the name Joseph-Marie as a novice in the Dominican order. At the age of eleven, he was diagnosed with a disease of the retina that was to lead progressively to total blindness. He felt an early calling to the priesthood, which he maintained in spite of official discouragement on account of his handicap and, having successfully completed secondary education, entered the Dominican convent in St Maximin, taking his vows as a monk at the age of twenty-four. Overcoming all the problems occasioned by his visual handicap, he was ordained as a priest, and in 1930 was posted to the Dominican convent in Marseilles. There, his ministry was largely on a one-to-one basis, a speciality of the Marseilles convent. He also worked with students and young people, notably the "Jécistes" ("jeunesse étudiante chrétienne"), and in 1936 founded what was to become the focus of much of his life's work, "Caritas Christi", a lay order of women dedicated to serving God in everyday life, under the patronage of St Catherine of Sienna.

During World War II and the Occupation, Perrin played an important role in the Resistance, organising the distribution of the clandestine newspaper *Les Cahiers du Témoignage chrétien*, and coming to the aid on a personal level of many Jews and others suffering Nazi persecution. In August 1943 he was betrayed by a double agent and imprisoned for two weeks, during which he was interrogated by the Gestapo.

After the war he travelled extensively in Europe, North America, Brazil, North Africa, supervising the development of Caritas Christi, accompanied by his secretary and collaborator, Solange Beaumier, who acted also as his "eyes" and generally organized his material existence, allowing him to lead a life of commitment that would not otherwise have been possible.

With her death in 1980, Perrin's activities were indeed severely curtailed, but he continued to write and to contribute to the Dominican community in Marseilles until his death in 2002 at the age of ninety-six.

Gustave Thibon

Born in 1903 in the Ardèche in southern France, Thibon retained throughout his long life an intense attachment to his rural origins. His father, a peasant-farmer and a man of considerable culture, passed on to his son his love of poetry, in French, Provençal and Latin, so that although Gustave Thibon was essentially self-taught, having left school at an early age, his childhood combined high culture with a respect for the values of the soil. As a youth, he travelled within Europe, learning English and especially Italian, and discovered North Africa during military service. The discovery of Nietzsche, whose writings became a life-long passion, added German to his familiarity with European languages and cultures.

By the age of twenty-three he was back in Saint-Marcel d'Ardèche, to devote himself to farming, and to reading, writing and reflection on literature and philosophy, creating works which were to be recognized by the 'Grand Prix de l'Académie Française' for literature in 1964, and that for philosophy in the year 2000.

World War I was a warning to him of the dangers of ideological patriotism and of all shades of fanaticism. It also sowed the seeds of his pronounced suspicion of democracy when contaminated with demagogy. Under the influence of the Catholic philosopher, Jacques Maritain, he converted to Catholicism, but remained an independent voice in regard to the Church and Church teachings. His attitudes reflected more closely therefore those of Simone Weil, whom he acknowledged as among those having had the greatest influence on his mature philosophy, than those of Maritain, a strictly orthodox thinker.

Gifted with a prodigious memory, Thibon's ability to quote from the various European languages he had mastered was legendary, and his culture grew more ample with the passing years. In his own writings, his preferred mode was the aphorism, open-ended and unsystematic, reflecting, however, a harmonious whole. Abhorring obfuscation, his style had a lucidity that belied the complexity of thought that lay behind it. He published his last work, a volume of memoirs, in 1993, at the age of ninety, and died in his native village in 2001.

J.P. Little

INTRODUCTION

by J.P. Little

With the death of Gustave Thibon on 19 January 2001 and that of Father Joseph-Marie Perrin on 13 April 2002, the final chapter in the story of their long relationship with Simone Weil has been concluded. Simone Weil's early death in 1943 brought the dialogue with her two friends to an abrupt end as far as she was concerned, but both Thibon and Fr Perrin continued to derive spiritual nourishment from their memories of the brief period of their dialogue with her in 1941 and 1942, and from those writings that she entrusted to them both on her departure from France on 14 May 1942 and others that began to appear after the second world war. It is appropriate, therefore, that this account of the relationship, first published in French a mere nine years after Simone Weil's death and in this English translation the following year (13),[1] should be offered again to the public.

Simone Weil's relationship with Perrin and Thibon spans a short but critical period in her development. The circumstances of their encounter are evoked briefly by both men in this volume, and in more detail elsewhere (see Bibliography): when Paris was occupied by the Nazis in 1941, Simone Weil, accompanied by her parents, fled south, arriving eventually in Marseilles, where she came across Hélène Honnorat, a young teacher and committed Christian, who introduced her to Father Perrin. Perrin, learning of her desire to work on the land, which was provoked in part by her exclusion from the teaching profession through the anti-Jewish laws then in force, spoke on her behalf to Gustave Thibon, a self-taught philosopher who farmed in the Ardèche. As well as spending a critical few weeks with the Thibon family, Simone Weil also saw Perrin on a regular basis while she remained in Marseilles.

1941–42 was clearly a traumatic year in French history. The fall of France in June 1941 seemed to have brought about the collapse of everything the country stood for, creating enormous disorientation, social distress, fear and hardship. Simone Weil's writings from this time until her death in London in August 1943 bear witness to her agonized response to the unprecedented crisis. The experience of the war turned her acute social conscience from its main pre-war preoccupation, the organization of labour, towards an analysis of why France had been defeated in this way, and an elaboration of the conditions necessary for its regeneration. Simone Weil's own personal destiny is therefore inextricably linked at this point with that of her native land. At the same time, however, she was undergoing a profound spiritual development, the details of which she did not reveal to anyone at this time. But her close association with a Catholic priest and a committed Catholic layman certainly played a major part in this development and, in the case of Perrin in particular, in the clarification of her position regarding the Catholic Church.

The relationship that was to develop was different in nature in the case of the two men. When Simone Weil approached Father Perrin, it was to a professional of the Catholic Church that she appealed. His role was to listen to and counsel individuals needing spiritual guidance, and in a sense he had no choice but to listen. He himself makes a distinction at the beginning of his Foreword (p. 13) between himself as a person and his mission. Simone Weil therefore looked to him as an authoritative voice speaking for the Church, and their dialogue reflected her assumptions. Thibon, on the other hand, could let their dialogue develop freely. The fact that it developed at all was due first to his overcoming, for reasons which he never quite understood, his initial reservations when asked to take into his household a young Jewish intellectual with a reputation for left-wing militancy and second to his acute insight into the inner nature of the singular personage who presented herself to him. In an interview in 1975, he noted that he has often been accused of promoting Simone Weil's writings out of friendship for her. In fact, he says, it was for directly opposite reasons: at the beginning, he felt no spontaneous friendship for her whatsoever, rather what he calls 'an alarming lack of sympathy'. He admits to having been 'conquered in spite of [him]self by the purity of that soul, the quality of that mind'.[2]

The friendship Simone Weil developed with both Thibon and Perrin is recorded for their part in the pages that follow, and in many of their other writings. The fact that we have a record of it from Simone Weil's point of view is due entirely to the hazards of war that provoked her exile and the consequent physical impossibility of continuing the dialogue face to face. She gives her account of it, although, it must be noted, not for the public eye, in the very beautiful and revealing letters to Father Perrin published as a part of Waiting on God (Attente de Dieu; 21, pp. 13–69) and in letters to Thibon which appeared more recently, along with his replies, in the *Cahiers Simone Weil* (22).

Simone Weil had a very high idea of friendship. She considers it to be one of the 'forms of the implicit love of God', described in the essay written in Marseilles and published under that title (*21*, pp. 154–61). The miracle of friendship is characterized by a sense of true equality between the two parties, and recognition of the autonomy of the other. It is devoid of any sense of need, dependence, or desire to please. The friendship that Simone Weil developed with both Perrin and Thibon clearly fulfilled these requirements and was indeed a manifestation of the love of God himself. 'Nothing among things human is as powerful' she asserts, 'as a way of keeping the gaze focused ever more intensely on God, than friendship for God's friends.'[3]

Assuming then this solid human bond, let us turn now to examine in more detail the development of the relationship first between Simone Weil and Father Perrin. Its direct expression is contained in the letters of *Waiting on God*. But other texts dating from this period were composed with Father Perrin in mind, or as collaborative projects. The essay 'On the right use of school studies' (*21*, pp. 71–80) was written for his students at the convent in Montpellier, where he was briefly posted, and the texts which were subsequently collected and published as *La Source grecque* and *Intuitions préchrétiennes* were designed for a much larger project in which they were to have collaborated, on Christian inspiration in pre-Christian societies. Simone Weil passed all these essays over to Father Perrin as she left Marseilles for the United States on 14 May 1942. She deeply appreciated Father Perrin's apparently boundless charity and his social concerns, and she showed a keen interest in several of his ventures. Perrin was also responsible for introducing her to the editor of the Catholic journal *Économie et humanisme*, and it was through him that she was able to engage in Resistance work with Marie-Louise David. There was clearly a very positive collaboration, therefore, in terms of their respective social consciences.

Their spiritual dialogue remained, however, at the centre of their relationship. There were misunderstandings at the beginning: when she approached him, Father Perrin asked her if she prayed, to which she replied in the negative. In fact, as she tells him later in her 'Spiritual Autobiography' (*21*, pp. 31–51), she had already had three highly significant 'contacts with Christianity', the latter two of which had involved a 'contact with Christ' that she recognized subsequently as prayer.[4] In the same letter, she evokes the deep sense of the presence of Christ that came frequently to her during her recitation of the Lord's Prayer in Greek, a practice she had adopted during her stay with Thibon, after, therefore, her first meeting with Perrin, and which she had confided to neither of her friends (*21*, p. 40). Simone Weil remained extremely discreet on the development of her spiritual life: the only other person in whom she confided on the subject was the invalid poet Joë Bousquet. Father Perrin had, however, the perspicacity to recognize Simone Weil's spiritual authenticity, although he knew nothing at this point of her mystical experiences, and in spite of the fact that he found her knowledge of Catholicism 'very inadequate' (*10*, p. 65)

There were other initial misapprehensions. Alluding to his 'love for Israel', he provoked a strong response from Simone Weil, who did not hide from him her aversion to the Old Testament (*10*, p. 65). But their most critical point of divergence, and the one that certainly tried the priest's patience most sorely, was the issue of the Catholic Church. Simone Weil's mystical experiences had brought her to the threshold of the Church: in many ways, she was deeply attracted by the idea of belonging to it through baptism, and she longed for participation in the sacrament of the Eucharist. But certain fundamental points held her back, centring mainly around the notion of the Church as an institution. In Simone Weil's interpretation, the Catholic Church was the direct descendant of the Roman Empire, the Great Beast of the Apocalypse, inheriting its lust for temporal power and totalitarian tendencies. She writes to Father Perrin of an 'insurmountable obstacle' to the true incarnation of Christianity, that is, the use of the words *anathema sit*, the formula by which heretics were excluded from the Church's sacraments. She was convinced that the mysteries of Christian dogma were objects of loving contemplation rather than affirmation or denial. She rejected also the Jewish inheritance of Christianity, and the concept of a chosen people, seeing in the Gospels the spirit of ancient Greece that she put on a higher level of spirituality altogether. Rejecting what she saw to be the exclusiveness of the Church, overwhelmingly conscious of all the generations before Christ and all the peoples who had not heard the message of the Gospel, she saw it as her mission to remain waiting (*en hypomene*), on the threshold (*21*, p. 40), or as the church bell summoning the faithful from the outside, as she told Thibon (*22*, p. 10).

Perrin clearly found this deeply troubling. In the various essays that he devoted to his dialogue with Simone Weil, of which the text in this volume is only one example, he returns again and again to the way in which he had tried to explain to her the 'errors' in her interpretation of Catholic teaching, and one senses his increasing frustration that she did not appear to comprehend. He clearly cannot understand how someone with such deep spiritual insight could remain so closed to the true nature of the Church. He also reproached her for some of her interpretations of

Biblical passages, and what was to him the cavalier fashion in which she juxtaposed Christian truth and pagan myth. While maintaining their friendship with great loyalty and recognizing her genuine spiritual gifts, his writings on her are frequently very critical of her views on the nature of the Church and Christian doctrine, and often appear to be largely a justification of Church teaching. Was this due to a sense of failure on his part? When a rumour began to circulate after her death that she had in fact been baptised *in extremis* by a friend in London, Simone Deitz, Perrin took the trouble to go to the United States to question her about it, and is one of the few people to attach importance to it, if it ever took place. Such a baptism would, after all, from his point of view, have been the crowning achievement of their relationship.

His placing of Simone Weil's baptism and consequent entry into the Church at the centre of their relationship is related closely to what Simone Weil herself discerned as a 'serious imperfection' in her friend, namely a certain partiality. She caught him one day, for example, referring to certain ideas as being 'false' when he meant 'unorthodox', indicating 'a confusion of terms incompatible with true intellectual probity', interpreting the cause of this to be his attachment to the Church as an 'earthly fatherland' as well as a celestial one (*21*, p. 64). It is to Perrin's credit that his regard for his outspoken friend did not diminish as a result of this criticism; it seems he took it as a manifestation of their mutual regard for truth, and he in fact included it in one of his subsequent essays. But it illustrates both a point of fundamental discord and its probable cause. It was without doubt this discord which caused his Preface to *Waiting on God* to be suppressed after the first edition. When he realized that Simone Weil's parents were concerned at any suggestion that he was trying to bring their daughter into the fold, he also abandoned a project to prolong their dialogue after her death by creating a research Journal dedicated to those who, like Simone Weil, sought spiritual truth.

The relationship between Simone Weil and Gustave Thibon was different in nature, but just as challenging and transforming. We have already evoked the unpromising nature of their initial contact; but Thibon readily concedes that after two or three days his initial impression had been completely reversed. Disagreeing radically on the temporal plane – Thibon having opted to support the Vichy régime, whereas Simone Weil was already totally committed to resistance – they soon discovered total communion on the level of spiritual reality. 'I have never met in a human being' asserts Thibon, 'such a familiarity with the mysteries of religion; never has the word *supernatural* seemed to me more full of meaning than in contact with her.'[5] According to him, it was a recognition of something other than himself, however, of qualities that he at that time did not possess. In a much later text, he admits: 'I was made to know Simone Weil and I had the good fortune to know her but, at the time when I met her, my level of spiritual evolution did not coincide with hers, so that our real dialogue began only after her death'.[6]

That dialogue is revealed as a passionate and wide-ranging exchange between two minds avid for nourishment, on the plight of France at that time and more generally on political ideas and the foundations of society, on literature, culture, the arts, religious ideas and the Catholic Church. Their views frequently conflicted – some of their differences in literary taste, and the reasons for them, are presented in Thibon's essay in this volume – but he maintains that when Simone Weil's opinions and excesses provoked a brutal contradiction or an exasperated silence on his part, she never manifested the slightest degree of hurt pride, and he quickly grew to feel only 'unconditional respect' for the singular being who had crossed his path so unexpectedly. In their political thinking, despite their differences over contemporary issues, they nonetheless shared a common perception that politics was the art of the lesser evil, and Thibon therefore found Simone Weil curiously tolerant in this area. As with Perrin, Simone Weil's dialogue with Thibon examined also her relationship to the Catholic Church. As he demonstrates in the following pages, he found her refusal to enter the Church when on the threshold – as she undoubtedly was, in his opinion – deeply problematic (p. 156). But he admits in the end to a lack of understanding of the forces which kept her on the threshold, at the same time as he denies any desire to try and 'convert' her after death. His approach to the subject, inevitably, is less strained than Perrin's. In his Introduction to *La Pesanteur et la grâce* – which, like Perrin's Preface to *Waiting on God*, was omitted after the first edition – he evokes two dangers in dealing with Simone Weil's relationship to Christianity: the first being to judge her thought in the light of strict orthodoxy, the second that of trying to make that thought coincide with orthodox doctrine. He declares his intention of avoiding both dangers.[7] In some respects, his view of the Catholic Church was similar to Simone Weil's: the Church partook of the nature of social reality, belonging not to absolute good, but to the realm of the necessary (*3*, p. 28).

This judgement on the Church reflects Thibon's beliefs on the nature of God, which often echo Simone Weil's. God, in the realm of appearances, is 'terribly absent'. He is above all 'an orientation'. Idolatry consists in 'looking for the eternal on the temporal plane and the infinite on the plane of the finite'.[8] While initially he was suspicious of Simone Weil's desire to 'return to the soil', he soon learned that they shared a common perception of work on the land being a contact with reality.

He refers to 'the realism of the land, that perpetual control of the idea by the facts'.[9] Simone Weil's evocation, in a letter to him, of the reward belonging to work on the land and to none other, that is to say 'the feeling that the land, the sun, the landscape truly exist and are something other than a decor'[10], must have struck a chord in him. It is neither possible, nor would it be helpful, to say whether such concordance of thought, here and elsewhere, is due to direct influence from the thought of Simone Weil. But it would seem that there were in Thibon similar tendencies, a similar commitment to the absolute and clear apprehension of the limitations of the temporal, which attained their maturity through contact with Simone Weil's thinking.[11]

Simone Weil herself was clearly aware of her friend's potential at the time of their brief meeting, but extremely lucid in her view that this potential had not yet been realized. In a passage of brutal frankness, she comments on writings he had submitted for her comments, noting that although 'they contain [. . .] some things of the highest order', these were 'not many; not nearly as many as the praise of your friends suggests': there was still much 'dark night' to be endured, before Thibon would give his 'true measure' (see pp. 123–24).[12] It says much for Thibon's lack of susceptibility that he accepted – and quoted – such criticism.

The period Simone Weil spent at Saint-Marcel d'Ardèche was thus one of growth on both sides. In Simone Weil's case, as we have already noted, it was not always expressed. But the bond was sufficiently close for her to pass over all the notebooks in which she had daily been elaborating her ideas, instructing him to do with them as he wished. She seems to have been expecting him to use them in the development of his own thought, and seemingly felt no personal attachment to them. 'It is certainly very preferable for an idea to link its destiny with yours rather than mine', she writes. 'I am not someone with whom it's good to throw in one's lot.'[13]

Thibon did not, of course, accept her suggestion that he should simply use her notebooks as a quarry for his own writings. *Gravity and grace (La Pesanteur et la grâce)* was the fruit of his editing of a selection of extracts from these notebooks, and because, apart from the various political and syndicalist articles which had appeared in specialist journals and newspapers during her life, it was the first glimpse the wider public had of this extraordinary writer, it conditioned the way in which Simone Weil was perceived. For Thibon, she was simply 'the greatest spiritual author of our times'[14], and he felt he was presenting her thus; but, given his deep Catholic faith, it was perhaps inevitable that *Gravity and Grace* suggested a less complex relationship with Catholicism than was actually the case.

While appreciating the complexity of that relationship, the reader of the pages that follow will not be tempted to question the reality of the friendship between Simone Weil and both Gustave Thibon and Father Perrin, nor their deep admiration for her spiritual gifts and her profoundly human generosity.

Notes:

[1] Italicized numbers refer throughout to the numbered sequence of the Bibliography. Superscript numbers refer to footnotes.

[2] *3*, p. 113: 'J'ai été en quelque sorte vaincu malgré moi par la pureté de cette âme, par la qualité de cet esprit.'

[3] *21*, p. 42: 'Rien parmi les choses humaines n'est aussi puissant, pour maintenir le regard appliqué toujours plus intensément sur Dieu, que l'amitié pour les amis de Dieu.'

[4] For these and other biographical details, see *14*.

[5] *15*, p. iii: 'Je n'ai jamais rencontré, dans un être humain, une telle familiarité avec les mystères religieux; jamais le mot de *surnaturel* ne m'est apparu plus gonflé de réalité qu'à son contact.'

[6] *16*, p. 33: 'J'étais fait pour connaître Simone Weil et j'ai eu la chance de la connaître mais, à l'époque de notre rencontre, mon niveau d'évolution spirituelle ne coïncidait pas avec le sien, de sorte que notre vrai dialogue n'a commencé qu'après sa mort.'

[7] *15*, p. xxv: 'Le premier [danger] consiste à confronter la pensée en question avec les principes de la théologie spéculative et à condamner sans pitié tout ce qui, vu du dehors, n'apparaît pas strictement orthodoxe. [. . .] Le second danger consiste à vouloir infléchir coûte que coûte la pensée qu'on étudie dans le sens de la vérité catholique.'

[8] *3*, p. 32: '[Dieu] est avant tout une orientation.' '[L'idolâtrie] consiste à chercher l'éternel au niveau du temporel, l'infini au niveau de l'indéfini.'

[9] Quot. in *2*, p. 131: 'Le réalisme de la terre [. . .] ce contrôle perpétuel de l'idée par les faits.'

[10] Letter to Gustave Thibon, *Cahiers Simone Weil*, IV, 2 (Jume 1981), p. 67: '. . . la récompense attachée au travail de la terre et à aucun autre, le sentiment que la terre, le soleil, le paysage existent réellement et sont autre chose qu'un décor.'

[11] For a discussion of the question, see Gabellieri, *arts. cit.*, especially XIII, 2 & 3: 'Les convergences'.

[12] For the original version of this letter, see *Cahiers Simone Weil*, IV, 2 (June 1981), 68–70.

[13] Letter to Gustave Thibon, *Cahiers Simone Weil*, IV, 4 (Dec. 1981), p. 196: '. . . il est certainement bien préférable pour une idée d'unir sa fortune à la vôtre qu'à la mienne. [. . .] Je ne suis pas quelqu'un avec qui il soit bon d'unir son sort.'

[14] *3*, p. 115: 'Je tiens Simone Weil pour le plus grand auteur spirituel de notre époque'.

Bibliography

1. Barthelet, P., *Entretiens avec Gustave Thibon*, 2nd edn, Paris: Edns du Rocher, 2000

2. Chabanis, Christian, *Gustave Thibon témoin de la lumière*, Paris: Beauchesne, 1967

3. ——, *Entretiens avec Gustave Thibon*, Paris: Fayard, 1975

4. Devaux, André-A., 'Joseph-Marie Perrin, guide spirituel de Simone Weil', *Cahiers Simone Weil*, XXV, 3 (Sept. 2002), 255–66

5. ——, 'Gustave Thibon et Simone Weil: une amitié sans complaisance et sans faille', *Cahiers Simone Weil*, XXV, 3 (Sept. 2002), 236–54

6. Gabellieri, Emmanuel, 'Simone Weil et Gustave Thibon' *Cahiers Simone Weil*, XII, 2 (June 1989), 140–48; 'Simone Weil et Gustave Thibon (II)', *Cahiers Simone Weil*, XII, 3 (Sept. 1989), 256–75; 'Simone Weil et Gustave Thibon II: les convergences', XIII, 2 (June 1990), 179–201; 'Simone Weil et Gustave Thibon II: les convergences (suite et fin)', 3 XIII, (Sept. 1990), 287–315

7. J.-M. Perrin, 'A propos de Simone Weil'; Appendix I to *L'Eglise dans ma vie*, Paris: La Colombe, 1951, pp. 117–24

8. ——, Preface to *Réponses aux questions de Simone Weil*. Textes de J. Daniélou, C. Durand, J. Kaelin, L. Lochet, B. Hussar, J.-M. Emmanuelle; Réponses de l'Eglise, Paris: Aubier, Editions Montaigne, 1964

9. ——, 'L'eau du baptême' (Interview with Robert Ytier), *Entretiens en marge du colloque de Sète (1979) sur les refus de Simone Weil* (Extract from a series of nine broadcasts on France-Culture, 28 April–9 May 1980), Paris: Association pour l'étude de la pensée de Simone Weil, 1982, 41–5

10. ——, *Mon dialogue avec Simone Weil*, Preface by André-A. Devaux, Paris: Nouvelle Cité, 1984

11. ——, 'Simone Weil et sa recherche profonde' *Cahiers Simone Weil*, XII, 3 (Sept. 89), 203–209

12. ——, 'Mon amitié avec Simone Weil', in *Comme un veilleur attend l'aurore* (Propos recueillis par Bénédicte Dubois), Paris: Editions du Cerf, Collection Signatures, 1998, 136–153

13. ——, and Thibon, Gustave, *Simone Weil as we knew her*, London: Routledge and Kegan Paul, 1953. Translation by Emma Craufurd of *Simone Weil telle que nous l'avons connue*, Paris: La Colombe, Edns du Vieux Colombier, 1952

14. Pétrement, Simone, *La Vie de Simone Weil*, Paris: Fayard, 1973, 2 vols. American trans. by Raymond Rosenthal, *Simone Weil: A Life*, New York: Pantheon Books, 1977

15. Thibon, Gustave, Introduction to Simone Weil, *La Pesanteur et la grâce*, Paris: Plon, 1948, i–xxxiii

16. ——, *L'Ignorance étoilée*, Paris: Fayard, 1974

17. ——, 'L'Univers religieux' (Interview with Robert Ytier), *Entretiens en marge du colloque de Sète (1979) sur les refus de Simone Weil* (Extract from a series of nine broadcasts on France-Culture, 28 April – 9 May 1980), Paris: Association pour l'étude de la pensée de Simone Weil, 1982, 6–11

18. ——, 'Le pouvoir de la littérature' (Interview with Robert Ytier), *Entretiens en marge du colloque de Sète (1979) sur les refus de Simone Weil* (Extract from a

series of nine broadcasts on France-Culture, 28 April – 9 May 1980), Paris: Association pour l'étude de la pensée de Simone Weil, 1982, 12–16

19. —, *Au soir de ma vie*, Paris: Plon, 1993

20. Weil, Simone *Attente de Dieu*, 1st edn, Preface, comments and conclusion by J.M. Perrin, Paris: La Colombe, 1950

21. —, *Attente de Dieu*, 2nd edn, Paris: La Colombe, 1950 (edition used in this Introduction)

22. —, and Thibon, Gustave, Correspondence, *Cahiers Simone Weil*, IV, 2 (June 1981), 65–74; IV, 3 (Sept. 1981), 129–38; IV, 4 (Dec. 1981), 193–200

SIMONE WEIL
as we knew her

J. M. PERRIN
AND G. THIBON

NOTE

Simone Weil wrote to one of us that friendship should not affect differences nor differences friendship.

This golden rule always dominated our relationships with her – perfect independence was preserved together with complete openness.

Faithful to this principle we here offer our testimony, combined yet separate, and each of us is only responsible for his own text.

INTRODUCTION

TO THE ORIGINAL WORK

Gustave Thibon

When a person, event or work meets with success or notoriety, it is generally found that the height reached by these modern substitutes for glory is in exact proportion to the vanity and impurity of their source. A scandal makes a greater sensation than an act of heroism, a boxer or film star attracts more attention than a great artist or a solitary philosopher, and, when fame does chance to descend upon true greatness, it is more than likely that there has been some misapprehension or mistake; either the greatness is not seen for what it is but triumphs under some disguise, or the 'glory' merely lights up that side of it which is showy, picturesque and, for that reason, superficial. Nietzsche said: 'When a great truth triumphs in the market place, you may be sure that a great lie has contributed to its victory.' That is the bitter and almost inevitable price of success. Who has written a book on 'The refusal to succeed'?

These disillusioned reflections are specially applicable to Simone Weil's great reputation. That she who instinctively rebelled against every kind of prestige and pretension should have become a social figure, the object of the noisiest and hollowest publicity – there we have one of those paradoxes which suggest that the counsels of Providence are not without irony. She wanted to live in the humblest obscurity. She considered all social privileges – money, rank, honours, influence, etc. – to be screens between the soul and reality, deceiving us as much as they promote our comfort. She saw them as a kind of padding made of illusions and preventing man from having real contact with

1

necessity in its naked truth. It was down on the rough earth at the base of the social pyramid that she felt nearest to heaven, and, when she chose to share the life and work of factory hands and farm labourers, it was perhaps chiefly in order to embrace all that is most dehumanizing in the lot of the very poor – anonymity and impersonality – seeing this as the best way to disappear from the eyes both of herself and of the world. Emptied of self by exhausting work, lost to view among the crowd, she hoped to attain to that mystical 'nothingness' which, here on earth, is the image and threshold of the All. 'The self', she used to say, 'is only the shadow which sin and error cast by stopping the light of God, and which I take for a being.' And now, by a strange reversal, her longing for self-effacement has defeated its own end, and only serves to bring out in greater relief the external characteristics of that self which it was the whole aim of her existence to destroy. The crowd, which is incapable of discerning the albatross's solitary flight across the sky, eagerly watches its more or less picturesque movements on the deck of the social ship, where its giant wings prevent it from walking'. A great deal of the flood of literature now appearing on the subject of Simone Weil abounds in superficial contrasts between the young bourgeoise graduate of philosophy and the anarchist, the factory-hand, the land girl and the volunteer on the Spanish front. Simone Weil has become renowned for her heroism and self-sacrifice – she has become a star with all that the word implies of artificiality and adulteration. A legend is growing up around her in which the picture of her life at Epinal encroaches a little too much upon the invisible reality.

Baudelaire wrote the following words – which are not so well known as they deserve to be – concerning the difficulties of giving an adequate account of the lives of the truly great in narrative form: 'Who could conceive a biography of the sun? From the time when the flaming ball gave its first sign of life the story is one of monotony, light and greatness.' And indeed, one can no more write the story of the sun than the story of God. What a condemnation of all that side of history which appeals to the depraved appetite of the crowd! The emptier a soul is, the less it is able to savour immutable essentials, and the more it needs the condiments of anecdote and novelty. We cling to the event at the expense of the substance, without dreaming that in all that is of deep value and authentic reality, in everything which has about it the simplicity of original light, being and happening, essence and existence tend to coincide. In the higher regions nothing appears to happen because what happens is always the same. The sun is reborn, identical and immaculate at each dawn, the rivers flow on for ever between the same banks, and so it is with the faithful love which binds two human beings together till death, or with the love of a God whom nothing can weary or discourage and who makes the rain to fall upon the just and the unjust. Not one of these great nutritive realities has about it any unexpected accident or sensational novelty capable of arousing public curiosity – that only comes as a result of some relatively superficial and unimportant occurrence. For instance, there may be an eclipse of the sun, the river may overflow its banks, the husband and wife may have a quarrel, or God may work a miracle in the material order. The deep reality is too eternal to be 'actual', too intimate and too continuous to be sensational. That is why it is not noticed. . . .

The true greatness of Simone Weil was of such an order. Depths of silence have to be traversed in order to grasp the authentic meaning of her words. Moreover it is no longer she who pronounces these words; it is the Spirit from above, into whose submissive instrument her body and soul are transformed; at those times of supreme inspiration the hand which writes and the mind which thinks have become nothing but a 'link between mortal and immortal', an impersonal intermediary through which the Creator and the creature exchange their secrets'.

Of such a Simone Weil – the confidante of universal love – it is better not to speak; her message absorbs her personality; her life, her character, her actions become as she herself expresses it 'infinitesimal to the nth. degree' – particles of chance in the bosom of an ocean of necessity. Biography can deal only with what is contingent, the absolute and universal provide no handle for narrative.

Simone Weil, however, like every created being, was not constantly and completely under the influence of supreme inspiration. Side by side with her deep originality – which dealt with the origin and consequently the Author of all things – and her purity which was invisible to the outward eye, she was gifted with another kind of originality in the relative order of appearances – an originality which was not only visible but striking, provocative, almost aggressive. And these two sides of her nature were not only juxtaposed, but were very closely interconnected. It was because she had placed herself once and for all in the eternal centre that she appeared eccentric in relation to the conventions of temporal and social life. Her thirst for the absolute generally led her to adopt one of two attitudes with regard to things of relative value. Either she exaggerated their importance and too easily lost sight of their imperfections and limitations, or else she overlooked them completely. Thus she wanted the State to make the study of Greek compulsory in all its schools, and at the same time one cannot say that she scorned (because scorn implies some previous knowledge), but she was completely unaware of most of the customs and conventions of social life, from the art of dressing oneself to that of pleasing. In both cases her fate was that of Baudelaire's swan – to be 'like exiles, ridiculous and sublime'. To tell the truth, whether it was a question of veiling the body or the soul, Simone Weil knew nothing of clothes and fashions, and that is why outwardly, both from the physical and moral point of view, she attracted attention and made such a sharp and disturbing impression. Like most of those who are marked by a transcendental vocation, she was at the same time above and below the level of normal activities, and the picturesque singularity of her person was at once the consequence and the antithesis of the self-effacement and transparency of her personality. There was always the same opposition and polarity between them as between the flight and the walk of the albatross. It is not necessary to repeat which of these two aspects is the more calculated to excite curiosity and create a legend. . .

There are two currents discernible today in the reception given to Simone Weil's message, and they can be roughly attributed to these two aspects of her personality.

The first, if I may say so, is of the nature of hagiography. Surprise at the original genius of her work, a legitimate admiration inspired by her utter purity, and the reverence due to the great dead, have combined in causing her message to be considered as a kind of infallible revelation of universal import. Man is so prone to idolatry that he readily imagines genius or heroism to constitute absolute guarantees against imperfection and error. From this point of view, any reservation appears to be out of place, any criticism almost a blasphemy. This results in the presentation of a deplorably flat picture of the being or the work unduly adored (what is more insipid than the work of most apologists?) for, in refusing to see the limitations of a human being, one is bound to miss his deep reality which is marked and as it were moulded in its very foundations by these same limitations. One substitutes a perfection, the frozen immutability of a mummy, for the warmth and movement of a finite human body. Much could be written about the sterilizing process of idolatry.

The second tendency is to stress everything which might be considered as exaggerated or illusory in the thought of Simone Weil in order to question, not only the deep value, but even the authenticity of her spiritual testimony.

Between these two extremes there are a host of interpretations – some profound but nearly all of them tending to isolate or restrict. They all seek to bring out this or that aspect of the philosophy or spirituality of Simone Weil while they lose sight of her constant effort to find a universal synthesis which, in spite of so many extreme and partial judgments, always remained the essential motive at the centre of her thought. It is thus that we have been presented with a Simone Weil reduced to Stoicism, pantheism, Platonism, anarchical individualism, anti-semitism, etc. No doubt in a sense she had all these tendencies; but she herself was something more, something different from them all, just as an organism cannot be identified with any of its members – nor even with their sum.

As opposed to these totalitarian, and for that very reason mutilating, interpretations, we here offer the testimony of two men who knew Simone Weil intimately and loved her as she actually was. We are opposed to all idolatry (positive or negative) and all that is exclusive with regard to her. Our attitude will be strictly determined by her own words on the love of creatures:

'The beings I love are creatures. They were born by chance. They will die. What they think, what they feel, and what they do is limited and is mixed with good and evil . . . I would know this with my whole soul and not love them the less. . . .' We must own quite simply that such lucidity in love, difficult as it is with no matter what created being, is specially so with such a one as Simone Weil. Naturally inclined to extremes, she almost automatically provokes extreme reactions in others. The finite and infinite, which paradoxically coexist in all men, in her case form contrasts so great and of such violence as to confound the judgment. Attracted by that in her which is infinite, one is tempted to forget her limitations, or else, shocked by her limitations, one is in danger of misunderstanding that which is infinite. We will try to avoid this double pitfall. There is no true fidelity which does not recognize in the person we love both greatness and misery – God the Creator and original nothingness.

Our testimony to Simone Weil will be on these lines. Moreover (and we say this in all sincerity and with complete conviction) we not only have the right to offer such a testimony, but it is our duty to do so.

The right, because each of us knew her intimately. The intimacy was short but deep. With one of us it was chiefly concerned with religion and the spiritual life, with the other it had more to do with daily existence and philosophic enquiry. Moreover, we knew Simone Weil when her interior life and her creative genius were at the height of their glowing maturity. It was the time of the supreme harvest in which God stoops down to gather the reaper as the latter is gathering his sheaves.

Besides the right there is the duty, for when Simone Weil left France during the war to go into the unknown, she confided the greater part of her writings to our special care, and she gave them to us, not just as a deposit, but as a possession which she asked us to use as we saw fit. There is nothing to suggest that in the secret of her soul she ever revoked this choice which had been determined by the mystery of sympathy grafted on to the chance of our meeting. This is a fact, and we state it as such, without vainglory or false modesty. It is possible that we did not deserve the absolute confidence Simone Weil placed in us. But every privilege is also a responsibility, every heritage entails a duty, and the only way to become worthy of it is to carry out what it demands of us. Simone Weil loved only the truth. The words of Gertrude von Le Fort, 'It is better to die of the truth which God has made than to live by the lies we create for ourselves', are more applicable to her than to anybody, and it is our duty to return the confidence she gave us during her life by presenting the truest and most faithful likeness possible after her death – not indeed with the 'objective' indifference of the scholar, but with the eager lucidity of a love which is too real and too exacting to surround itself with illusions.

However faithful it may be, our testimony is bound to be incomplete. First because we only knew Simone Weil during a short period of her life. Secondly because the reserve which necessarily accompanies intimacy does not permit us to say everything. Transparent as were the soul and life of Simone Weil, all friendship worthy of the name has in it regions which cannot be revealed: the deepest part of all we might say about her – all that touches upon the experiences and secrets we shared – that is just what we will never divulge! But this very intimacy, though in its own order it is sacred, diffuses an indirect light which enables us rightly to appreciate and interpret certain episodes in her life and elements in her writings. Those who judge from outside see everything spread out on the same plane; the most diverse texts, once they are written down, are given equal importance; two opposing assertions neutralize each other, etc. But he who, through an experience of friendship and life in common – and in such experience intensity counts for more than duration – is able to judge from within, can make, as it were, deep cross-sections of his friend's work. In this way he is enabled to distinguish what is essential from what is accidental, the life-giving sap from the bark, the vital elements from the epidermis or even the mere clothing! He possesses a fragile, subtle but irreplaceable criterion, authorizing him to separate what is deep and enduring from what has but a superficial, passing significance in the words which those lips now silent have left us. What commentator of Plato, for instance, would dare to bind in the same sheaf the highest texts of the *Banquet* with certain absurd lucubrations of the *Republic*?

Yet it was Plato himself who said sadly of the written word: 'Its father is no longer there to defend it.' But in that case does not the task of its defence devolve upon the friends of the 'dead father', upon those to whom he confided what was in his heart and who dispose of his inheritance?

These considerations have all the more weight if we remember that the greater part of Simone Weil's work came to us in the rough, without being shaped and prepared for publication. How is it possible to know in what manner this or that hasty note or judgment without context corresponded with her thought? How, in this uneven mass of material, is it possible to distinguish that which is based on deep, unshakable conviction from that which is no more than verbal extravagance, provisional theory, too hasty generalization, polemical effect, irony, or even just a reminder jotted down with a view to some future train of thought which she never developed. In the exploration of such a labyrinth, the guiding thread issuing from past intimacy and communion, though not necessarily infallible, is of the greatest help.

At this point a very serious objection comes up. 'Both of you are convinced Catholics,' we are told. 'Is there not a risk that faithfulness to your Church will weigh more heavily in your judgments than faithfulness to Simone Weil's memory? In other words, impregnated as you are with Catholic doctrine, will you not always be unconsciously tempted to bend Simone Weil's thought in the direction of your faith, to minimize the differences which separate her from you and magnify the affinities?

Our reply is clear as day. Simone Weil knew what we were, what we thought, what we believed. Yet, not only did she entrust us with the task of publishing many of her writings, but she invited us to use them as we chose and to incorporate them in our own work. She could thus have foreseen the spirit in which the sorting and arrangement of the material placed in our hands would be carried out. After all, the choice of two Catholics for the diffusion of her thoughts can scarcely have been the result of chance or a mere whim: it does at least prove that the possibility of a Catholic interpretation did not in any way shock her. In declining this offer, which was as generous from her point of view as it was impossible for us to accept, we are convinced that we have not gone as far as she would have allowed us – or perhaps as she would have wished us to go.

This does not in the least mean that we feel ourselves to have the exclusive right of interpreting Simone Weil. Quite the contrary! The more uncalculating the giver, the more scrupulously careful the recipient has to be. Should we therefore lay aside our Catholicism in studying Simone Weil? That is neither possible nor desirable. Simone Weil does not ask us to deny our own beliefs in order to achieve that scientific objectivity which views all things from outside, but to become more deeply ourselves, that is to say more deeply Catholic in the etymological sense of the word, so that we may achieve the supreme objectivity which loves all things from within. In so far as we approach this ideal – which is, alas, so much beyond us – our Catholicism, instead of cramping our faculties of understanding and sympathy, infinitely widens our vision and dilates our heart; we have no need of those instruments – as complicated as they are inexact – by which human wisdom tries to measure out truth and falsehood, good and evil; all that is good and true comes to us spontaneously, and the rest disappears of itself, like mist in the sunshine or dust swept by the wind. We are too apt to forget that every Catholic is by definition the reverse of a partisan. If in reality he often becomes one, it is because he regards his faith as belonging to himself personally, or to a social group, and not as the domain of God. Thus, in serving his God whom he unconsciously transforms into a social leader, he is tempted to employ all the tainted methods which promote the existence and prosperity of parties, and, first and foremost, the great propaganda lever of lying. The mere thought of using such methods in connection with Simone Weil fills us with horror. More than our veneration for her memory, more than our own self-respect, our adoration of a transcendent and infinite God puts it out of the question. Such a God has no need of any person. We do not have to draw Simone Weil to him; she belongs to him already in so far as truth dwells within her. From this point of view, our Catholic faith constitutes the best possible guarantee of the absolute independence of our judgment. We know better than anyone what attracted Simone Weil to the house of God and what kept her on the threshold: it is graven for ever in our heart by countless shared joys and all too many painful discussions. . . . It is for God alone to fathom the mystery of this soul and her destiny. For our part, we will confine ourselves to bearing witness to 'what our eyes have seen and our ears have heard', and also to 'the feelings which rose in our heart' when we were with Simone Weil. The testimony will necessarily be partial (in the sense of being incomplete), but we shall try also to keep it impartial, and, as we offer it to all those who have come or will come to Simone Weil through us, we are mindful of the fact that at their origin love and truth have but one name.

Part One

by J. M. Perrin

Simone Weil
in
Her Religious Search

FOREWORD

It is impossible to understand a conversation without listening to both speakers; it would be unjust to judge its full significance and to accept its testimony apart from such a context; that is why as more and more of Simone Weil's thought is made known I feel impelled to undertake this work, which is in a sense a marginal accompaniment to *Waiting on God* and *Intuitions Pré-Chrétiennes*.

Unfortunately it is impossible after the passage of years – and what years they have been! – to recreate a dialogue which was spread over ten months and which was not coloured by any external happenings.

The setting was practically always one of the bare, shiny parlours of the Dominican convent at Marseilles; the subject was always the great preoccupation which had first brought Simone Weil to me.

In terms which would overwhelm me if I did not know that they do not apply to me personally but to my mission, she has said what these meetings meant to her and what she found in our intercourse. It is not for me to return to the subject, but I must insist, now that thousands of readers have broken in upon our conversation with their prejudices and problems, their superficiality or their profundity, that what she said then represents her thought.

Time in its inexorable justice will show the value of her work, but since so many of our contemporaries are passionately interested in her testimony and spiritual experience, I should like to try to describe more fully than is possible in a preface – a preface is always too long – the development, or rather the 'waiting', of Simone Weil.

I have no preconceived opinion as to the outcome of that development, although I am more in a position to judge it now than I was a year ago.

It is true that the publication of her later writings has posed many problems and baffled more than one of her admirers; a thousand interpretations, favourable or antagonistic, and even some of my own formulæ, have combined to increase the tangle. Everyone has pulled the thread that suits him, and this is one of the things against which I think it is my duty to protest; no one has any right to misrepresent the thought of Simone Weil, either by distorting it, or by using it as a cloak for his own prejudices.

Facts are facts, and truth cannot gain through any misunderstanding. I know the value of the unique confidences she gave me, but I also know the agonizing sense of incompleteness which tormented her. I will not even try to say how far she was from Christianity – that remains a mystery – but I will merely redescribe the orientation of her thoughts and the subject matter of our conversations.

I can do this more easily now, since the publication of *La Connaissance Surnaturelle* has brought out the importance of certain pages of *The Need for Roots* and since the *Letter to a Priest* has given, not so much an enumeration of her real difficulties, as an account of one of the tendencies of her spirit and of the inward conflict which rent her. I can do it still better since the unpublished papers she wrote in London have been communicated to me through the extreme courtesy of Monsieur Maurice Schumann – writings which form what is perhaps the most vigorous expression of Simone Weil's soul during the last months of her life.

Precious as these documents are, they are subsequent to the months in Marseilles and are therefore outside the subject to which I feel I should confine myself.

As for that period – in addition to my personal memories and the testimony of a few friends, I have had the good fortune to find some notes and several passages of hitherto unpublished letters of Simone Weil; the correspondence with G. Thibon supplies some very exact information about her deepest thoughts, and, at least once, about her reactions after we had had an interview.

The texts which have appeared under the title *Intuitions Pré-Chrétiennes* belong to the same period. They are all covered by our conversation, and even form one of the most essential parts of it. They show how deeply Simone Weil was concerned to find Christ in pre-Christian times, and especially in Plato. Were these texts to solve the problems raised so many centuries ago by the philosopher? Do not Plotinus and Saint Augustine both stem from him? Specialists will admire her very extensive knowledge of ancient Greece, but will they share this interpretation? That is their business. From my own point of view these pages throw important light on Simone Weil's religious quest.

To complete this documentation, I must mention the three articles belonging to the same period which appeared in the *Cahiers du Sud* under the signature of Émile Novis (an anagram of her name).

I have left nothing out so that I may be as objective as possible and reduce to a minimum all chances of error or of a refraction of memory due to the passage of time.

As for the spirit of this essay, it is the same as that which always inspired our conversations: a spirit of attentive listening for the truth. Should it be possible, justifiable and perhaps necessary to pass an abstract judgment and to refute an impersonal error by supra-personal arguments, it would further be necessary, in order to be just and objective, to make an effort to understand the sense of the words used and their bearing in a system different from our own.

I could never attempt to do this, however. I am always conscious of a very living person and of a mind whose sense of the incompleteness of its own thought I am perhaps better able to measure than anyone else. A Christian is the disciple of a master who did not wish to crush the broken reed . . . above all the 'thinking' reed.[1] I am mindful of the words which Saint Augustine addressed to the Manicheans although he was acutely aware of their perfidy and their errors: 'May those upbraid you who do not know how much labour is required to find the truth, and how many difficulties have to be overcome to avoid error!

May those upbraid you who do not know how rare and hardly-won is the triumph of serenity over carnal imaginations in a soul which has found peace in piety! May those upbraid you who do not know how difficult it is to cure the inward eye and enable it to look fixedly upon its sun – not the sun you worship which the eyes of men and animals behold, but that of which the prophet wrote: "The Sun of Justice shall arise" (Mal. iv, 2), of that of which the Gospel says: "That was the true light which enlighteneth every man that cometh into the world" (John i, 9). May those upbraid you who do not know at the price of how many sighs and groans we attain to a knowledge of God, however feeble and partial it may be. May those upbraid you, in short, who have never been misled by an error such as they detect in you (Migne, P.L., xlii, col. 174).

I have seen too many souls labouring with doubt in their arduous quest, I have seen too many struggling with inexplicable misunderstandings, not to realize with what respect we should approach them. Of course I know that there are too many who do not love the truth because their works are evil, but none of us know how far we ourselves or any others share this condemnation.

We only truly hate error when we love those whom it deludes; the Augustinian injunction to combine the love of persons with the hatred of vice is obligatory. 'Truth without charity is an idol.'

Besides, do we not refute an error best by showing what it contains of truth? The tarnished reflection will only shine if it is brought back to the light from which it emanates. My Greek master used to love to repeat to us the far-reaching maxim that every error is 'a broken ray of truth'.

We save an idea by freeing it from its falsifications and perversions in order to bring it back to the truth, rather than by fighting against it – just as we save a soul by bringing it back to God. In his own infinitesimal way the Christian, like Christ, knows that he is sent not to judge but to save.[2]

I will therefore try to give a faithful account of the ideas and the searchings of Simone Weil, showing what were the causes of her inner conflict and the directions in which she might have found the peace of truth in charity.

Simone Weil as I knew her, and as I shall try to portray her, still remains all that is truest – superior to the fragmentary writings which have appeared under her name and which are in the nature of preliminary sketches, produced while she knew herself to be in a state of evolution and incompletion. In order to understand her and not to reproach her for her contradictions, her gropings and her oscillations, it has to be remembered that she does not provide us with a solution but a question: not a reply, but an appeal; not a conclusion, but a need.

J.M.P.

Notes

[1] Cf. Pascal: 'Man is but a reed, the most feeble thing in nature, but he is a thinking reed', *Pensées*.

[2] This, indeed, has always been the spirit of the Church. Plus XII expresses it in the following words: 'The Church has never scorned and disdained pagan doctrines, but she has freed them from all errors and impurities, and then completed and crowned them with Christian wisdom.'

I.

BIOGRAPHICAL NOTES

Simone Weil, faithful to her principles, scarcely ever spoke to me about herself, her childhood, her family or even her political or social activities. She said in a letter to me that friendship 'is not really pure unless it is so to speak surrounded on all sides by a compact envelope of indifference which preserves a distance' (Letter IV). Deep as was her friendship, she strove to keep it impersonal. It may be useful, all the same, to recall briefly the main features of a biography already known to many of my readers. Simone Weil was born in Paris on 3rd February 1909. She received no religious education: 'I was brought up by my parents and my brother in complete agnosticism,' she wrote to me (Letter VI). Yet one could almost say that her outlook was Christian from the start. 'I might say that I was born, I grew up and I always remained within the Christian inspiration' (Letter IV).

One of her dominant characteristics as a child was a compassionate love for those in misfortune. 'From my earliest childhood I always had the Christian idea of love for one's neighbour' (ibid.). During the 1914 war, when she was only six, she went without sugar in order to send all her share to the soldiers who were suffering at the front. When she was nine or ten, the anti-German reaction which followed the Treaty of Versailles made her into a Communist (Letter to Bernanos).

Striking, also, was the precocity of her intelligence which enabled her to win every kind of scholastic success. On the advice of a friend, she went to the Lycée Duruy for her year of philosophy in order to be taught by Le Senne. She prepared for the competitive entrance examination of the École Normale at the Henry IV where she was deeply influenced by Alain. She was nineteen when in 1928 she entered the Normale, and twenty-two when in 1931 she passed out as an *agrégée* (or qualified teacher) of philosophy. During the months spent at the École she showed herself to be thoroughly '*antitala*',[1] she was even anti-religious enough to quarrel for several months with a friend who was about to become a Catholic. It was at this period that she came into contact with the trade union movement and the *Révolution Prolétarienne*. Afterwards she continued to support these movements, but without joining any party. She never spoke to me of the important people she had occasion to meet or help, or of the part she was called upon to play; she knew my point of view: while a priest is in sympathy with all that makes for human progress, yet he is bound to keep out of politics as far as possible. Moreover, in her own case it was surely a love for the oppressed and suffering that predominated. A young working man who was one of her companions in these social struggles said to me: 'She never went in for politics', and he added: 'If everyone was like her, there would be no more destitution.' It seems now that many of her former companions have deserted her on account of her spiritual evolution; I think that she, on the other hand, remained faithful to them. In any case this part of her life deserves special attention from her future biographers – through it they will discover one of the essential aspects of her inner life.

Her first post was at Le Puy: there she began to give free expression to her compassion, that real communion with the hardships and suffering of others. In order to have a right to the unemployment dole, the workmen were set to very heavy tasks; she saw them breaking stones and wanted to take her share with a pick-axe. She accompanied them when they went to present their case at the Prefecture. She reached the point of spending no more on her own needs than the daily sum allowed by the dole, distributing everything else she had to the unemployed. Thus it came about that on the day when the young teacher of philosophy received her salary, a procession of her new friends was to be seen beseiging her door. Later on, she even carried her delicate sympathy – perhaps one of the most beautiful of her characteristics – so far as to give generously of her time, time snatched from the books she loved so passionately, in order to play their favourite card game of *belote* with some of these friends, to have a try at singing with others, and to become in every way one of themselves.

Simone was far from feeling satisfied, however. Compassion is torture for anyone who truly loves. That is why in 1934 she decided to embrace the workers' lot in its utmost severity. She knew hunger and weariness, the rebuffs and tyranny of work in a chain factory, the agony of being unemployed. It was never just an experiment with her but it was a real and total self-giving. Her 'factory diary' is a poignant testimony. The trial was beyond her strength; her soul was, as it were, crushed by this consciousness of affliction: she bore its mark for the rest of her life. 'After my year in the factory . . . I was, as it were, in pieces, soul and body. That contact with affliction had killed my youth. Until then I had not had any contact with affliction, unless we count my own, which, as it was my own, seemed to me to have little importance, and which, moreover, was only a partial affliction, being biological and not social. I knew quite well that there was a great deal of affliction in the world, I was obsessed with the idea, but I had not had prolonged and first-hand experience of it. As I worked in the factory, indistinguishable to all eyes, including my own, from the anonymous mass, the affliction of others entered into my flesh and my soul. Nothing separated me from it, for I had really forgotten my past and I looked forward to no future, finding it difficult to imagine the possibility of surviving all the fatigue. What I went through there marked me in so lasting a manner that still today when any human being, whoever he may be and in whatever circumstances, speaks to me without brutality, I cannot help having the impression that there must be a mistake and that unfortunately the mistake will in all probability disappear. There I received for ever the mark of a slave like the branding of the red-hot iron which the Romans put on the foreheads of their most despised slaves. Since then I have always regarded myself as a slave' (Letter IV).[2]

When the Spanish war broke out in 1936 Simone, who had strongly supported the strikes then going on (articles in the

Révolution Prolétarienne), did not hesitate to leave for the Barcelona front: an accident due to her lack of manual dexterity (she scalded herself with oil) caused her to be evacuated almost immediately. Simone scarcely ever referred to this part of her life except to speak of one or other of her comrades in arms. Her recently published Letter to Bernanos seems to be the best source of information about this period of her existence and about the deep impressions it left with her.

In 1938 she spent Holy Week at Solesmes and the great illumination which was to change her life followed a few months later: 'Christ came down and took possession of me.' It is difficult to determine the exact date of this experience for she guards the secret of it jealously; there is no mention of it in any of her private papers and, as far as I know, she did not confide it to any of her friends, apart from what she said in her letter to Jö Bousquet and what she told me by word of mouth or by letter. One thing is clear – in the midst of the gropings of her search and the oscillations of her thought, she never lost her sense of it: in the light of this unknown experience, she had a new outlook on the world, its poetry and its religious traditions.

Then came the war. She did not leave Paris until after it had been declared an open city. It was then that she arrived in Marseilles. The anti-Jewish regulations affected her. In June 1941 she came to see me and in one of our first conversations she spoke to me of her wish to share the work of the agricultural labourers. I could see quite well that this was not just an unconsidered impulse but a deep decision. It was then that I asked Gustave Thibon to help in the scheme. Thus she spent several weeks in the Rhône valley and knew the arduous toil of grape-harvesting.

How can I describe these months in Marseilles? As I have already said, she spoke little of herself and her activities, yet, in spite of herself, how could she pass unnoticed? I shall speak elsewhere of her spiritual evolution.

As regards her literary activities, she was in contact with the circle of the *Cahiers du Sud* and wrote several important articles for this publication under the pseudonym of Émile Novis; notably 'L'Iliade ou le poème de la force' (The Iliad or the Poem of Force), 'L'agonie d'une civilisation vue à travers un poème épique' (The Death Agony of a Civilization seen through an Epic Poem) and 'En quoi consiste l'Inspiration occitanienne' (That which Constitutes Occitanian Inspiration), not to mention several poems. Besides this, the best part of her time was given up to her translations from Homer and from the writings of the Pythagoreans, which appeared under the title *Intuitions Pré-Chrétiennes* (Pre-Christian Intuitions), and to the composition of the essays which form part of *Attente de Dieu (Waiting on God)*. She used to read these texts to a few friends who came together for intimate little gatherings at which she tried to communicate her love of Greece and above all of the realities reached by the great mystics.

It is rather remarkable that the books she chose for reading at this period were the *Mémoires* of the Cardinal de Retz and the *Tragiques* of d'Aubigny.

Reading and writing did not fill her life: the bent of her mind and the compassionate will which characterized her made it impossible for her to remain detached from the life of the most unfortunate of her fellows. She sought them out and mixed with them in order to know and help them. She was specially interested in the Annamites who had been demobilized and were waiting to be repatriated; realizing the injustice of their fate, she managed so cleverly that she had the commandant of their camp superseded.

On one occasion this love of her fellows saved her life. She had been arrested as a Gaullist, and after a long interrogation she was threatened with prison 'where she, a teacher of philosophy, was to be put with prostitutes'. Thereupon she made this sensational reply: 'I have always wanted to become familiar with such circles and the only way I could ever see of gaining admission to them myself was this – going to prison.' At these words the judge made a sign to his secretary and she was released as mad!

Since we have now come to the time of the underground movements, it is to be noticed that Simone devoted herself to the spreading of *Témoignage Chrétien*: of all the movements existing at that time, it was the one she preferred. Later on, in order to persuade the authorities to parachute her into France, she stressed the fact of her contacts with its organizers. This is how she wrote of it: 'I think that it is by far the best thing in France just now. May no harm come to it.'[3]

Her great preoccupation, however, was always the religious question. She searched the Gospel for long hours, discussing it with her friends who used to love to find her at the Sunday Mass. She came to see me frequently, and in order to have greater solitude, she would sometimes come to an early Mass on a weekday. Did she not write to me at this time: 'My heart has been transported for ever, I hope, into the Blessed Sacrament exposed on the altar' (Letter IV). This sentence tells us much concerning the attraction which the living silence of our churches had for her!

Thus the weeks and months passed quickly in Marseilles. In March I was nominated for Montpellier. This somewhat complicated the arrangements for our last meetings, but provided the occasion for her most beautiful letters. She embarked with her parents on 16th May 1942.

On reaching New York she made use of all her contacts and all her former friendships in order to be recalled to London; she suffered at having left France as though she had been guilty of desertion and sent out appeals such as the following: 'I beseech you to get me to London, do not leave me here pining in sorrow'; 'I appeal to you to rescue me from the unendurably painful moral situation in which I am placed'; 'I beg of you, if you can, to procure for me the quantity of sufferings and dangers needed to save me from being worn out by grief in sterility. It is impossible for me to live, placed as I am at present. It drives me to the very edge of despair.'

All the same, her love for the disinherited of this world did not fail. 'I am exploring Harlem,' she wrote to one of her friends; 'I go every Sunday to a Baptist Church of Harlem where, except for myself, there is not a single white person.' She got into touch with the black girls, she invited them to her home, and this same friend, who knew her well, told me: 'It is certain that if Simone had remained in New York she would have become a negress!'

Yet her heart was given to the universe: 'The affliction spread over the surface of the terrestrial globe obsesses me and crushes me to the point of destroying my faculties, and I can only revive them and free myself from this obsession if I myself have a large share of danger and suffering. It is therefore necessary that this condition should be fulfilled if I am to be enabled to work' (to M. Schumann).

When she arrived in London at the end of November 1942 it was a bitter disappointment for her. She had only one aim: to be given some arduous and dangerous mission, to sacrifice herself in some useful way, either saving lives or carrying out some act of sabotage. She asked for this by word of mouth, she persisted in her request by writing: 'I cannot help having the shameless indiscretion of beggars. Like beggars all I can do in the way of argument is to cry out my needs. . . .' It was not wise to consent to her demand. She was employed on special brain work. Thus she spent long hours in her office, often eating nothing but a sandwich, staying on in the evening and, when she had let the time for the last train pass, sleeping bent over her table or stretched out on the floor.

While she was persistently begging for the longed-for 'mission', she noted down: 'My efforts here will soon be stopped by a threefold limit. First, a limit in my morale, for the agony of feeling that I am not in the right place will end, I am afraid, in spite of all I can do, by impeding my thought. Then a limit in the intellectual domain; it is clear that at the moment of coming down to what is concrete, my thought will stop for lack of an object. The third is the physical limit, for tiredness is increasing.'

Events proved her to be right, alas! In April the reality had to be faced and she was forced to give in. She was admitted to Middlesex Hospital. The treatment which she received there could not cure her on account of her extreme weakness. This was due both to exhaustion and privations. She longed for the country and was allowed to be moved to the sanatorium at Ashford, where she died on 24 August 1943.

Notes

[1] In École Normale slang *tala* means pious, *antitala*, free-thinking, from 'allant *à la* Messe'.

[2] *Waiting on God*, pages 19–20.

[3] Correspondence with M. Schumann.

Extract from a letter to the Reverend Father Perrin, published in *Waiting on God* (Letter III).

Translation:—

'I shall not be able to help thinking with keen anguish of all those whom I shall have left in France, and of you in particular. But that also does not matter. I think that you are among those to whom, whatever may happen, no real harm can ever come.

Distance will not prevent my debt to you from increasing day by day as time passes. For it will not prevent me from thinking of you. And it is impossible to think of you without thinking of God.

Do believe in my filial friendship,

Simone Weil

P.S. You know that for me there is no question in this departure of an escape from suffering and danger. My anguish comes precisely from the fear that in spite of myself and unwittingly, by going I shall be doing what above everything else I want not to do – that is to say running away. Up till now we have lived here very peacefully. If this peace is destroyed just after I have gone away, it will be frightful for me. If I were sure it was going to be like that, I think that I should stay. If you know anything which might throw any light on what is going to happen, I count on you to tell me.'

Je ne pourrai pas m'empêcher de penser avec une vive angoisse à tous ceux que j'aurai laissés en France, et a vous particulièrement. Mais cela aussi est sans importance. Je crois que vous êtes de ceux à qui, quoi qu'il arrive, il ne peut jamais arriver aucun mal.

La distance n'empêchera pas ma dette envers vous de s'accroître, avec le temps, de jour en jour. Car elle ne m'empêchera pas de penser à vous. Et il est impossible de penser à vous sans penser à Dieu.

Croyez à mon amitié filiale
Simone Weil

P.S. Vous savez qu'il s'agit pour moi de tout autre chose, dans ce départ, que de fuir les souffrances et les dangers. Mon angoisse vient précisément de la crainte de faire en partant, malgré moi et à mon insu, ce que je voudrais par dessus tout ne pas faire — à savoir fuir. Jusqu'ici on a vu se sont tranquille. Si cette tranquillité du paraissait précisément après mon départ, ce serait affreux pour moi. Si j'avais la certitude qu'il doive en être ainsi, je crois que je resterais. Si vous savez des choses qui permettent des prévisions, je compte sur vous pour me les communiquer.

II.

EVIL AND REDEMPTION

Perhaps the depth and resonance of a soul is never so well revealed as by its first contact with grace – by the virgin sound which the initial impact of divinity draws from it. Born to complete agnosticism Simone Weil did not wish to consider the problem of God. She was afraid of making a mistake which in such a matter seemed to her to be the greatest possible evil. Does not this fear in itself show the deep holiness of her soul? 'As soon as I reached adolescence I saw the problem of God as a problem of which the data could not be obtained here below, and I decided that the only way of being sure not to reach a wrong solution, which seemed to me the greatest possible evil, was to leave it alone. So I left it alone, I neither affirmed nor denied anything' (Letter IV). One of her old pupils told me that she refused to mention God in her philosophical teaching, saying that one does not speak of a subject about which one knows nothing.'

Her year in the factory placed her at the very centre of human distress. The acuteness of her intellect, her sensitivity, her lack of manual dexterity and of physical resistance, above all her constant headaches, reduced her to the wretched state she described to me (cf. Letter IV), and it was then that she first guessed that Christianity provided an answer to this misery. 'In this state of mind, and in a wretched condition physically, I entered the little Portuguese village, which, alas, was very wretched too, on the very day of its patronal festival. I was alone. It was the evening and there was a full moon. It was by the sea. The wives of the fishermen were going in procession to make a tour of all the ships, carrying candles and singing what must certainly be very ancient hymns of a heart-rending sadness. Nothing can give any idea of it. I have never heard anything so poignant unless it were the song of the boatmen on the Volga. There the conviction was suddenly borne in upon me that Christianity is pre-eminently the religion of slaves, that slaves cannot help belonging to it, and I among others' (Letter IV).

Three years later at Solesmes, in spite of splitting headaches ('each sound hurt me like a blow'), she followed the moving liturgy of Holy Week and found a pure and perfect joy in the unimaginable beauty of the chanting and the words. This experience enabled her by analogy to get a better understanding of the possibility of loving divine love in the midst of affliction; the thought of the Passion of Christ entered into her being once and for all (cf. Letter IV).

A little later came the great discovery: 'I felt in the midst of my suffering the presence of a love, like that which one can read in the smile on a beloved face' (Letter IV). In the account she gives of it to Joë Bousquet she insists still more on the link between intense physical suffering and this love which she did not think she had the right to name: 'A presence more personal, more certain, more real than that of a human being, inaccessible both to the senses and the imagination, analagous to the love which shines through the tenderest smile on a beloved face. . . . The result has been that the irreducible amount of hatred and repulsion bound up with suffering and affliction has been entirely turned back upon myself – and it is a very large amount, because the suffering in question is ever present at the very root of every thought without exception' (Letter to Joë Bousquet, *Cahiers du Sud*, No. 284). No doubt she insists upon this because Joë Bousquet was a great invalid who had been crippled in the 1914 war and had spent long years in bed.

For her, therefore, the discovery of God and the experience of affliction are indissolubly linked. In this she outstrips her masters, the Stoics, and is nailed to the very centre of Christianity. She had a supreme contempt for any form of wisdom which could not face affliction; she considered those apologetics which avoid it to be vain – without noticing that nevertheless, the divine condescension deigns to call each one by name; the Magi through a star and the good thief from a cross. Affliction was one of the subjects which she was always ready to discuss.

As a metaphysician and a mathematician she was indignant at all those puerile representations of divine mercy which failed to place it in its relation to affliction. After having imagined the most atrocious situations, she adds in one of the notes published by Thibon: 'I should tend to have an abiding conception of the divine mercy, a conception which cannot be effaced and which does not change whatever event destiny may send upon me, a conception which can be communicated to no matter what human being' ('Atheism as a Purification' – *Gravity and Grace*).

She often dwelt on the impartiality of God who makes his sun to rise upon the good and bad alike, but she did not free herself sufficiently from her philosophical conceptions. This prevents the Christian reader from feeling quite at home and gives rise to one of those conflicts in the centre of her thought which we shall be discussing further on.

Simone had a keen realization that the beauty of the world can only be revealed to those who have understood its incomplete and limited character. She said: 'All created things refuse to satisfy me as ends. This is the extreme mercy of God towards me. And that very thing constitutes evil. Evil is the form which the mercy of God takes in this world' (Introduction to *Gravity and Grace*). 'The world must be regarded as containing something of a void in order that it may have need of God' ('To Accept the Void' – *Gravity and Grace*).

The necessity of the world which constitutes its beauty as in 'the ever moving folds of the fugitive waves' or in 'the almost eternal folds of the mountains' leads us to God. 'This obedience of things in relation to God is what the transparency of a window pane is in relation to light. As soon as we feel this obedience with our whole being we see God' ('The Love of God and Affliction' – *Waiting on God*).

One of the points to which she often returned, and on which we were less in agreement, concerned Christian hope, which she refused to present to those in affliction. 'We should not speak of the Kingdom of God to those in affliction, for that is foreign to them, but only of the Cross' (*Connaissance Surnaturelle*, page 26). To be sure she is right in the sense that an imaginative representation of divine blessings is in danger of being corrupted by resentments and the lowest cravings for compensation; all apocalypses, except that of the Apostle, are there to express what daily experience suggests; we meet with distressing debasements of Christianity; but our Lord, who knows men's hearts, has insisted too much on his promises for us to ignore them – though in our contemplation we must preserve the mystery with which he surrounds them. Christianity is catholic in this sense also, that it has to help the weakness of little ones and beginners just as fosters the purity of the more perfect.

We shall be considering this subject again, together with others of a like nature, for here we have one of the aspects of Simone Weil's interior problem. Kind and merciful as she was, she would sometimes tend to make the exacting demands of a merciless logician: 'It is a good thing that you are not God,' I used often to say to her. She repeated this remark to other friends, who used it after her death in an article about her (*Cahiers du Sud*).

Profound and beautiful as these reflections on evil and affliction are, and deeply as they bear the stamp of her personality, they do not seem to me to constitute that which is most personal in Simone Weil. Affliction came to mean, for her, experience of the love of God: 'It is in affliction itself that the splendour of God's mercy shines; from its very depths, in the heart of its inconsolable bitterness. If still persevering in our love, we fall to the point where the soul cannot keep back the cry "My God, why hast thou forsaken me?", if we remain at this point without ceasing to love, we end by touching something which is not affliction, which is joy; something which is the central essence, necessary and pure; something not of the senses, common to joy and sorrow; something which is the very love of God.

'We know then that joy is the sweetness of contact with the love of God, that affliction is the wound of this same contact when it is painful, and that only the contact matters, not the manner of it. . . . But we know quite certainly that God's love for us is the very substance of this bitterness and this mutilation.

'I should like out of gratitude to be able to bear witness to this' (Letter VI).

She did bear witness to this truth (of which she spoke to me several times) in *L'Amour de Dieu et le malheur* (The Love of God and Affliction); a paper which she gave me just as she was leaving and which some people consider to be her finest work. At the same period, in a more polished literary form, she tried to express the 'Christian light' which she felt in the *Iliad*. This is the theme of her article on '*L'Iliade* ou le poème de la force'[1] (*Cahiers du Sud*). Some people, who have attacked her without taking the trouble to understand or even to read her, have imagined that she confused the religious inspiration of Christianity with the divinities of Olympus whose role is less exalted than that of the heroes in the great epic – we shall be returning to this subject. In the light of God, she dwells on the sufferings of the innocent, recorded on every page. 'The poet of the Iliad loved God enough to have the capacity [to recognize Him in suffering]. This indeed is the implicit signification of the poem and the one source of its beauty. But it has scarcely been understood' (Letter IV).

For her own part, Simone Weil sought to fix her attention on those in affliction; if there is much in her writings concerning trials and accused, judges and convicts, it is because she often went to the law-courts, not out of curiosity but from 'compassion' and in order to contemplate affliction; we know the supernatural meaning underlying such an attitude in her case.

The cross had become for her the clearest manifestation of the love of God: 'God created through love and for love. God did not create anything except love itself, and the means to love. He created love in all its forms. He created beings capable of love from all possible distances. Because no other could do it, he himself went to the great-est possible distance, the infinite distance. This infinite distance between God and God, this supreme tearing apart, this agony beyond all others, this marvel of love, is the crucifixion. Nothing can be further from God than that which has been made accursed' (*The Love of God and Affliction*). Sin in reaching Christ becomes suffering and hence expiation: sin destroys itself by this operation. Here she liked to recognize the function of the 'Just servant of Isaiah and of the Lamb of God'.

In the same way, none of the proofs of Christianity and of the divinity of Christ had so much force for her as this one. 'The Cross is enough for me. The proof for me, the thing that is miraculous, is the perfect beauty of the accounts of the Passion, together with some brief passages of Isaiah and Saint Paul. That is what forces me to believe' (*Letter to a Priest*).

This unpublished fragment adds nothing to what is essential in her ideas, but it sums them up and shows their connection. That is why it is worth quoting. 'For the man who has understood with all his soul that everything is obedient to God, everything will be beautiful? God is absolute goodness: how can obedience to goodness be anything but beautiful? Such a man discerns in all that exists and all that happens, the mechanism of necessity, and he thinks of necessity as obedience.

'There are two kinds of obedience to God, voluntary and involuntary, and all the thickness of the creation which God has put between himself and himself, being as contrary to God as anything real can be, is without understanding and is subject to involuntary obedience.

'Involuntary obedience can only be mechanical necessity. For it is entirely exterior and this quality constitutes mechanical necessity. Each infinitesimal particle of matter is absolutely docile to all external pressure.

'There would be a chaos in which no reasonable being could exist if, as Plato says, necessity had not been conquered once and for all by the persuasion of wisdom. This blind mechanism, made of chance, produces the rhythm of day and night, the changing seasons, the trees and flowers. It produces all these without knowing. Yet it itself produces them. God has entrusted creation to necessity. Otherwise God would be within the process – here on earth and not in heaven. His presence would then bring all creation to nothing – or else God himself would not be goodness.

'Everything beautiful in the world is the trace of the persuasion of wisdom which has conquered necessity. All the blind destruction which comes about bears witness to the fact that this conquered necessity still rules and that God does not dwell here on earth but in heaven.

'What greater joy can there be for us, knowing from constant experience what we are, than to think of God as infinitely far away from us? With the impurity of our hearts, we should degrade God himself if he were near us here on earth and if he were not beyond our reach. He is in heaven and whatever evil we do, or whatever evil we bear, we know that no evil will be caused to God by it. All the evil that we see happening around us confirms us in the certainty that God is elsewhere, beyond our reach. Can there be a greater joy for him who loves, than to say to himself: "Whatever happens, he whom I love is in complete security"? Only those who love God have this joy.

'But if we are cruel enough to wish to have him whom we love with us in our distress, we also have this comfort full of pain. There is a point in space and time which contains God nailed, emptied of divinity and in the form of a slave.'

Note

[1] 'The Iliad or the Poem of Force', published in the Wind and the Rain, Spring, 1950.

III.

THE QUESTION OF BAPTISM

Simone Weil was gifted with a sense of affliction and redemption, a sense which she never ceased to deepen by loving meditation. In everything else she seems to have been in a state of evolution – I might even say of oscillation – except for a few points which we shall discuss later.

Our conversations constantly returned to the central question of baptism, but it would be quite wrong to imagine them to have been in any way systematic. Throughout the ten months of our contact, except during the weeks she spent at Saint-Michel-d'Ardèche, she used to come to see me as often as it was possible for both of us to fit it in. This depended more particularly on my own engagements, because her enforced holiday left her plenty of leisure – leisure which she spent as I have already described. With her extreme consideration for others, she used to wait quietly in the passage, letting two or perhaps three people pass before her. After they had gone we talked for whatever moments remained. On a few rare occasions she asked me to see her at a friend's house in order to have more time and freedom of spirit.

The convent was often invaded at that time by people who were being tracked down and were in need of help, shelter or passports. . . . The resulting difficulties in the way of our meeting did not trouble her, for she always preferred to be guided by necessity, especially where friendship was concerned. This did not make for a continuity in our exchange of ideas.

A few notes, the writings published in *Waiting on God*, translations from Plato and commentaries on his work, together with a few fragments, which luckily bear on our subject and elucidate it, are all that remain of our meetings. Since the publication of *Waiting on God*, I have been able to supplement my memories with a certain amount of fresh material, particularly Simone Weil's correspondence with G. Thibon.

The question of baptism came up very soon, but until now I have not sufficiently dwelt upon it since, for me, it goes without saying, baptism is not only rebirth by Water and the Spirit, it is also the sacrament of faith; if a catechumen asks for it or a priest gives it, this implies the recognized acceptance of the teaching of Christ presented by his Church: 'He that believeth and is baptised. . . .'

Therefore, when I speak of baptism as the central subject of our conversation, I am not attempting to define Simone Weil's spiritual position with regard to this sacrament, or others to which it gives access, so much as her position with regard to the faith of the Church. At first she did not seem to be aware of any problem. Her love of Christ seemed to be enough for her, and the extremely superficial idea she had of the Church and Catholics was not of a nature to suggest the slightest question in her mind. (In January 1942 she was to speak of 'the six or seven Catholics of genuine spirituality' whom she had chanced to meet in the course of her life, and at this period she had already found three or four at Marseilles!) When she had discovered the meaning of prayer, when she had caught a glimpse of the eucharistic mystery, when she had begun to understand the doctrinal depth of Catholicism, she began to face the question in all seriousness. Then she was prepared to reconsider most of the ideas which prevented her from entering the Church. It was on this subject that she wrote to me: 'As for the existence of a compact body of dogmas which are beyond thought, I think that this compact body is something of infinite price. But I think that it is offered to the attention rather than to belief. When in such a body one has clearly perceived points of light, one must remember that the dark parts most often appear to be so because one has not looked at them with enough attention. I say "most often" because there is also the inevitable effect of the human tendency to misrepresent, and therefore there must also be non-inspired parts;

but one must always be careful not to be mistaken in such matters. In this compact body, it is necessary to look at the dark parts until one sees light issue from them, but, before this happens, the only acceptance one owes them is that of attention itself. I mean the most intense kind of attention, that which is accompanied by love and which is indistinguishable from prayer. If there had not been a compact body of this kind, one would only look at what one already saw to be light, and thus no progress would be made.

'There are passages in the Gospel which used formerly to shock me and which I now find extraordinarily luminous. The truth that I find in them, however, is not in the least like the meaning which I formerly thought I saw there and which used to shock me. If I had not read and re-read them with attention and love, I should not have been able to arrive at this truth. But neither should I have been able to arrive at it if I had abdicated my own opinion, if I had made an act of submission with regard to them before I saw the light which they contain. Other passages from the Gospel are still closed to me; I think that, with time and with the help of grace, attention and love will one day make them also transparent. The same thing holds good for the dogmas of the Catholic faith' (unpublished fragments).

At times she envisaged the possibility of baptism and, whatever she may have said, the question was often in her mind. It was then that she went to see at least two priests that I know of in order to find out whether their doctrinal demands were the same as mine or whether the power of suggestion which she feared so much in friendship was not causing her to see the Catholic faith in too favourable a light. At other times, on the contrary, she thrust the idea of baptism aside for one reason or another; we will return to this subject, but, in speaking of her during these months, it is necessary to bear in mind this flux and reflux, otherwise our conversation cannot be understood. Her side of it must be seen against the background of a series of conflicts which on some days were painfully apparent but which were always latent and which gave her thought and her deeper life the character of incompleteness which made me choose the title of *Waiting on God*.

On my side, knowing both her will which was so obviously led by God and her scrupulous independence, my whole effort was directed to keep her in a state of readiness and moreover to bring her face to face with truth. She herself said to me: 'You have never advised me anything but to hold myself in readiness, and I am infinitely grateful to you for this' (unpublished fragment).

IV.

FAITH AND PHILOSOPHY

We are familiar with the Augustinian idea that words are vessels which do not cease to be pure and precious even when they are employed to convey the poisoned wine of error. Could we not turn it the other way round and admire the wine of grace even when it is poured out of imperfect or misshapen vessels, even when the human intellect has been deformed by a faulty philosophy or inaccurate ideas? In reality this is applicable to every man who tries to utter God's thoughts; we are more conscious of it, however, in the writings of those who have been swept off their feet by some great revelation; of those, above all, who are still groping in a state of transition. Sometimes the novelty of their expressions and the unaccustomed use to which they put the words they employ give a certain youthful directness to their testimony. Sometimes, again, their clumsy attempts serve to throw into greater relief the divine wisdom to which they aspire. But it may also happen sometimes that the opposition of their old ideas and former expressions hinders their ascent and obscures their conclusions. Has this been sufficiently recognized in the case of Simone Weil?

The light from which she gained her sense of a living, personal God and of Christ as the centre of revelation – this most beautiful light – fell upon an intellect impregnated with a completely different philosophy and culture, an intellect which had been formed by methods of thought and experiences of an opposite nature. Brought up on Stoicism and Platonism, Simone Weil would have been predisposed to see religious sensibility as the supreme blossoming of human life. The whole trend of her thought was in this direction. But an entirely contrary truth was borne in upon her; the light came down from on high; she received the certain knowledge that it is not man, but God, who is the measure of all things. She, who had enclosed herself in agnosticism, was given the power to come out of her prison; that is what she calls faith – supernatural love. Hence a certain amount of conflict between her faith and her philosophy.

We often spoke of God and of the attempts of theology to express his incomprehensible being in human terms. I remember explaining to her how, for Saint Thomas, God is joy, and how his love for himself is the principle of his love for his creatures – thoughts which she eagerly assimiliated. I may say in passing that that is why her assertions concerning the 'Roman God', the 'God of slavery' (*Need for Roots* and *Connaissance Surnaturelle*), gave me a painful surprise, for she did not even have the excuse of ignorance.

To come back to Marseilles: certain notes on which she was working enable me to affirm that she accepted the dogmas of the Church concerning God, the Trinity, the Incarnation and even the Eucharist. Often, however, when she wanted to express them herself, she had only imperfect formulæ at her command, even though a kind of genius prompted her in the use of them.

She insisted so much on necessity in divine life and on its impersonal character that she left one wondering how much liberty and spontaneity remained in the supernatural order; she confused the truth which comes from God and that which man can discover for himself: 'The geometry of the Greeks and the Christian faith sprang from the same source.' Far from seeing an opposition between science and religion she was inclined to confuse them even while she took pleasure in repeating in one of her favourite formulæ that man cannot take a single step in the vertical direction. Returning to an idea we had often discussed, she wrote later that 'the true mysteries of the Faith are themselves absurd, but their absurdity is such as to illuminate the mind and cause it to produce in abundance truths which are clear to the intelligence' (*Need for Roots*). She was always indignant at a misunderstanding of the supernatural which could lead people 'to take Bergson for a Christian – the man who thought he saw in the spiritual energy displayed by the mystics the perfect expression of that *élan vital* which he had turned for himself into an idol' (*Need for Roots*).

God for her was always he who had imposed himself upon her, either by contacts or experience – he who had 'come down' to her and whom she loved: I am quite sure that there is a God in the sense that I am quite sure that my love is not an illusion' (*Gravity and Grace*).

Still influenced by Spinoza in her difficulty to conceive or at least to formulate the meaning of transcendence, she saw creation as a withdrawal of God: 'For God, creation did not consist of an expansion but a withdrawal of himself. He ceased "to command" wherever he had the power to do so. . . . The creation, the Passion, the Eucharist – always this same movement of withdrawal; this movement is love' (*Connaissance Surnaturelle*). Such expressions are not free from exaggeration, but out of them Simone drew her conception of humility seen as a *decreation* through love, an effacement before God in order that once more he should be all.

Insisting on the other hand upon the impersonal character of God, she attacked puerile conceptions of Providence and certain popular formulæ concerning miracles, forgetting, or pretending to forget, that, in the Church, there is a theology, a wisdom which, amidst all the stammerings of human intelligence, strives to remain open to divine Wisdom. The complete faith which would have made Simone into a disciple of Christ would have given her access to this wisdom: 'Believe, and you shall receive understanding' (Saint Augustine).

V.

THE CHURCH, MYSTICAL
AND SOCIAL

Although in Simone Weil the conflict between the certitude of religious experience and her philosophical mentality went very deep and was of a universal character, only the initiated were aware of it. There was another more visible and more important conflict which held a predominant place in our conversations from the very fact that I strove to keep all our discussions within its orbit and not to allow them to stray to matters of secondary importance.

When Simone Weil came to see me in 1941 she defined her position as being 'on the threshold of the Church' at the nearest possible point for one who was still outside. This was a real illusion on her part. She was very far from Christianity, and seemed to be extremely ignorant on many points. She had no liking for religious practices and sacraments and was too easily satisfied with the ideas she had received on these matters in anticlerical circles. At the best she saw an irreducible opposition between the mystical order centred on God and the social order ruled over by 'The prince of this world'.

Without being resolved, this conflict was considerably atten-uated while she was at Marseilles. I tried to show her the fullness of life which Christ offers to us in the heart of his Church: I told her what he said to us about 'the Father who seeth in secret', and about his manifestation of himself to his own. The great mystics are there to show that the Spirit has been given to us for all time. How is it possible to oppose what is welded and fused together in the same fire?

The Gospel revealed to her this marvellous birth by Water and the Spirit. From the first we talked together of the means which Christ instituted for the communication of his life to us: 'You once said to me at the beginning of our relationship some words which went to the bottom of my soul. You said: "Be very careful, because if you should pass over something important through your own fault it would be a pity"' (Letter IV). Some weeks later, she discovered prayer: 'The infinite sweetness of this Greek text [the "Our Father"] so took hold of me that for several days I could not stop myself from saying it over all the time. A week afterwards I began the vine-harvest. I recited the "Our Father" in Greek every day before work and I repeated it very often in the vineyard. . . . The effect of this practice is extraordinary and surprises me every time, for, although I experience it each day, it exceeds my expectation at each repetition' (Letter IV).

On her return to Marseilles a little later, she had a revelation of the Eucharist in the convent church (incidentally this church is neither quite new nor altogether ugly!): 'He [the divine Spirit] led me into a church. It was new and ugly. He said to me "Kneel down." I replied "I have not been baptised." He said "Fall on your knees before this place with love, as before the place where truth abides" I obeyed.' (Prologue, *Connaissance Surnaturelle*).

She returned to the subject of the attraction she felt for the Eucharist in her confidences, and in May she wrote to me: 'Only now my heart has been transported for ever, I hope, into the Blessed Sacrament exposed on the altar' (Letter IV). She strove to realize the meaning of the eucharistic bread; some of her statements are faulty but they show the profundity of her religious enquiries; she came back to the subject in the unpublished notes she made in London: 'Through a convention established by God between God and men, a morsel of bread signifies Christ's person. It follows from this that since a convention ratified by God is infinitely more real than matter, the reality of bread, while still remaining, becomes simply appearance in relation to the infinitely more real reality which constitutes its signification. . . . A divine ratification necessarily implies a direct revelation from God and perhaps it may even necessarily imply the Incarnation.'

In London she continued to feel the attraction of the Eucharist just as she had in Marseilles: 'I may perhaps be in error, but in that case I must be the prey of a demon of an unheard of variety, a demon who drives one to seek nourishment in the spectacle of the Mass.'

During her stay at Marseilles she also began to discover the place of Our Lady in the worship and life of the Church. For a long time already she had been in the habit of repeating the *Salve Regina* as a beautiful poem, but, now that she had a better understanding of the place of the Blessed Virgin in the divine plan, she hastened to search for something equivalent in all the religions of humanity. Above all she meditated upon the deep meaning of Our Lady's vocation, and following her inward bent she loved to contemplate it as 'creaturely obedience', the most perfect readiness to carry out God's will.

At the same time she discovered the profundities of the Catholic faith by contemplating their harmony and beauty. She had difficulty however on account of a certain rationalism which the great discovery of Christ had not removed. She understood that 'they are realities', that 'they are of a higher order', that 'the only part of human intelligence which is capable of real contact with them is the faculty of supernatural love'; but she refused to envisage them as matters to be affirmed or denied, and thus as matters which could be laid down by the decrees of the Church.

Since they are realities, to assent to them is to subscribe to the truth and to deny them is to be in error, thus the formula are the subject of affirmation or denial. Simone caught a glimpse of this at times. She saw the necessity 'for the Church to preserve the Christian dogma in its integrity like a diamond, with incorruptible strictness' ('Le Génie d'Oc' – *Cahiers du Sud*, page 157). She accepted the Church as 'the guardian of the truth' against which the gates of hell shall not prevail; but, in spite of everything, there was always a somewhat pejorative implication in the very name of the Church for her, due no doubt to deeply rooted prejudices.

What then is the Church which she does not like? How can she compare it with the Beast of the Apocalypse?

When we take from the Church all that she says she loves in it, 'God, Christ, the Catholic faith, the Saints, Catholics of genuine spirituality, the Catholic liturgy, hymns, architecture, rites and ceremonies. . . . ', what is really left? Our individual and collective sins . . . and the prejudices which she never lost.

This text must be reread if we are to understand the meaning the words bear when written by Simone Weil, and perhaps we shall be more struck by the force of the passage and her lack of information if we remember that the rough copy did not include either the sentence concerning the Saints or that concerning the six or seven Catholics of genuine spirituality': 'I love God, Christ and the Catholic faith as much as it is possible for so miserably inadequate a creature to love them. I love the Saints through their writings and what is told of their lives – apart from some whom it is impossible for me to love so fully or to consider as Saints. I love the six or seven Catholics of genuine spirituality whom chance has led me to meet in the course of my life. I love the Catholic liturgy, hymns, architecture, rites and ceremonies. But I have not the slightest love for the Church in the strict sense of the word, apart from all these things that I do love' (Letter I).

She never ceased to feel the attraction of grace, and the fact that in May she was still speaking to me about baptism – adherence to Christ in his Church – shows how deeply her conscience was torn.

She wrote to G. Thibon: 'You must have guessed that Father Perrin's words yesterday evening greatly troubled me. They almost gave me the impression that I had not been quite straightforward with him, though I have always tried to tell him the truth. The thought that I might disappoint him and thus cause him any pain is extremely distressing for me because of my affection for him, and because I am grateful for the charity which leads him to desire my good. Yet I cannot enter the Church in order to avoid causing him pain. . . .

'I never quite understand what he is speaking of. When he spoke of "communicating to me the fullness of the Lord", was he thinking of that which only saints and those who come near to sanctity possess? But it cannot in any case be the property of the sacraments to confer that, for no one has ever said that the sacraments in themselves bestow sanctity. If he were to baptize me this evening, I think that tomorrow I should be almost as far from sanctity as I am at this moment; obstacles far more difficult to overcome than non-participation in the sacraments separate me from it. But if Father Perrin was speaking of such communication of God as any convinced Catholic has received, I do not think that in my case this has still to come. It is the same when he speaks of "the fold"; if this term is given the Gospel meaning of the Kingdom of God, I am unfortunately very far from it. If it is of the Church that he is speaking, it is true that I am near to it, for I am at the door. But that does not mean that I am ready to enter. It is true that the slightest impulsion would be enough to make me enter; but there must be an impulsion, otherwise I may remain indefinitely on the threshold. My great anxiety to please Father Perrin cannot take the place of this impulsion, but can only make me hold back in order to avoid an illegitimate mixture of motives.

'At this moment, I should be more ready to die for the Church, if one day before long it should need anyone to die for it, than I should be to enter it. To die does not commit one to anything, if one can say such a thing; it does not contain anything in the nature of a lie.

'Unfortunately I have the impression that I lie whatever I do, either by remaining outside the Church or by entering it, if I do enter. The question is to know where there is less of a lie, and this is a question which is still in suspense in my mind. It is unfortunate that precisely on this point I cannot ask Father Perrin's advice, for I cannot put the problem before him as I see it.

'I so long always to give pleasure to the people I love, and it is always my destiny to be a cause or an occasion of pain.'

What exactly had I said to her? My joy to see the light growing within her? My hope that her search should be crowned and her waiting satisfied? Besides, whatever she may say, she had often asked my advice on this subject and I had repeatedly told her that the disposition required by any sacrament is an abandonment to the Spirit's influence irrespective of any human consideration. It is no more permissible to ask for a sacrament in order to please someone than it is to administer it for that reason. The purely objective requirements of the sacramental order oblige a child of the Church to rise above his personal point of view and to see everything from the point of view of Christ.

Moreover, as the value of the sacraments comes from Christ's institution of them and action through them, it does not depend upon our personal appreciation but requires the opening of our souls to God and obedience to him.

A few months later, in *Connaissance Surnaturelle*, Simone returned at some length to the subject of the Church. She dwelt on the corruption of true religion as symbolized by the Beast of the Apocalypse, but she also dwelt on the presence of Christ in the Church through the Eucharist, on the guardianship of the truth, on the Our Father and on the sacraments (pages 79, 261, etc.). When she invented a history of Catholicism, she forgot that Rome is not the capital of Christianity because of Cæsar or Augustus, but because it was there that Peter and Paul bore witness with their blood. When she saw 'Roman superstitions' as the cause of all corruption, was she not over-simplifying the question, for a falling away from religious purity is surely a natural and universal malady of our poor humanity? When she bravely asserted (*The Need for Roots*, page 265) that 'apart from pure mysticism Roman idolatry has defiled everything', was she not forgetting the liturgy, the rites and the ceremonies which are the official formula of Catholic prayer made available without distinction to all the faithful? I remember, in contrast to her, a young convert who, because he wanted to know the Church from inside before entering, meditated at great length on the Missal; nothing better shows the Church in its truth than its way of addressing God.

Simone was always torn by this conflict. Yet a truth which she discovered when working on Provençal Inspiration might have helped her to resolve it: 'We must not have any love other than charity. A nation cannot be an object of charity. But a country can be, as an environment bearing traditions which are etermlal' (*Gravity and Grace* – 'The Great Beast'). In connection with the *Langue d'Oc* and the song of the Crusades, she marvelled at the notion of language, or speech as they then called it, which, without any political union, economic bonds or treaties, had the power to bind people indissolubly together and make them risk everything in a war without hope. For them the same speech stood for a common culture and outlook, a heritage from the past and a sharing of the same values.

I leave it to scholars to say how much historical truth there is in this conception, but the conception in itself might have enabled her to see the Church as the 'Word of Christ' and the language of the Holy Spirit. If the human means utilized by the Church have their own nature or gravity – as the Incarnation limited God's human presence in space and time – this does not prevent them from having a divine value by virtue of the grace and truth of God which they convey.

How could charity fail towards the Church, which is the soul's home and the Father's house here on earth? That is what the Church is, coming as it does from God and leading to him by virtue of his institution, his promises, and his presence.

There may be suffering for those who have understood this, but there cannot be conflict.

We may love the Church badly, in a narrow way, making ourselves the centre or reducing it to our own views; we may love it erroneously, either by seeing only the social reality (as in positivist apologetics) or, on the other hand, by going to the opposite extreme and recognizing only its spiritual reality. We cannot love it too much if we love it in truth 'following the example of Christ who loved it and gave his life for it'. This synthesis can only be achieved in the Pentecostal Fire, by the gift of the Spirit who has his own times and secret workings; we can only say God's words in a human fashion and when these words enter the soul in accordance with God's grace and with our own liberty.

We have, moreover, to remember two things when we read Simone Weil's attacks or reservations with regard to the Church: she always confuses the reality with those distortions of it which she specially dislikes, and further, she is all the more severe in her judgments the more nearly a being or institution touches her.

As regards distortions, two examples come into my mind: the collective spirit and doctrinal authority.

Simone's culture and philosophy and the anarchist leanings of her past life gave her a strong dislike for any kind of collectivism. Under these circumstances how could she fail to entertain a very lively hostility towards any collectivity which was oppressive – oppressive, moreover, in the name of God? But the Church is not like that, even if some people have tended that way through exaggeration, either in Catholic Action or in liturgical matters. The Church has repeatedly declared, notably through Pius XII a few months before Simone's death, that it is at men's service and exists to minister to souls, that is to say to the human person as an absolute entity in relation to God: it serves this relationship and helps man to go to God. The Church never ceases to teach this incommunicably personal relationship with Christ, and what Simone says against the conception of the mystical body is quite misdirected, or is directed against certain distortions which the Church deplores even more than she herself could have done. Here are the actual words of the encyclical:

'Every human society in so far as one considers the final purpose of its usefulness, is directed ultimately towards the greater good of each and all of its members, for they are persons. That is why as the Son of the everlasting Father came down from heaven for the eternal salvation of us all, so he has founded this body which is the Church, and he has enriched it with the divine Spirit in order to give immortal souls the means of attaining their bliss according to the words of the Apostle: "All things are yours. And you are Christ's. And Christ is God's"' (I Cor. iii. 23. Pius XI, *Divini Redemptoris*. Quoted in *Mystici Corporis Christi*).

A convert, well known for the penetration of his soul and his inclination to subjectivism, noted down the following thought on this subject in his journal: 'Apart from that unparalleled community which is the Communion of Saints, all collectivism is a myth, and if the Communion of Saints is quite the contrary, it is because it is a community of non-interchangeable souls, each of them being unique and all of them being united to God, and having over them none but God' (Ch. Du Bos, *Journal de février*, 1939).

As for doctrinal authority and the formulæ taught by the Church, Simone had caught a glimpse of the solution, but was wrestling with problems and difficulties coming from her university education under Alain and from her philosophic conceptions. She saw no connection between subjective ideas which leave us shut up within ourselves and are controlled by our intelligence, and the power to come out of ourselves which she conceived of as purely supernatural and which she called 'faith', 'charity'.

The Church on the other hand asserts – and Saint Thomas has formulated the assertion with force – that dogmas are given us in order that we may reach divine reality. 'I have called you friends: because all things, whatsoever I have heard of my Father I have made known to you' (John xv. 15). They are nothing more nor less than the formulation of divine confidences. If I may be allowed to make the comparison, they are not like photographs or maps, but like windows through which the faithful can look – dimly but truly – at divine reality; they are the 'inexhaustible treasure. Whoever acquires them has a share in divine friendship' (*Wis.*, VII, 14). The affirmation and negation contained in these formulæ have reference to the actual object of faith and give a divine assurance to our obscure view. The authority of the Church is of the same order as that of the Holy Spirit; the same Spirit speaks in the Church and in the secrecy of the soul, and this Spirit leads both to the same object; the Church is gifted with infallibility only in order to make absolute the soul's adherence to the truth, which it should love and by which it should live until the time when it can contemplate it face to face.

Simone Weil's difficulty in this matter was not peculiar to her: it is often found at the present time among those who do not understand that man's intelligence is made for the truth itself and not for subjective representations of this truth. This difficulty is common to all who oppose dogmatic formulæ to mystical intuitions, whereas, for the enlightened Christian, the revealed Word – formulated in dogma – is the way of approach to God; it is faith which becomes increasingly penetrating and clearsighted.

Or again, the formulæ of faith are like musical scores which express the divine harmonies by human signs. Some people scarcely get beyond the difficult reading of this musical manuscript which faith, full of mystic wisdom, enjoys with tireless wonder. The formula is correct even when little understood and badly played, and it expresses the harmony of the divine mystery of which the mystic already has a presentiment without any human analogy.

We can therefore no longer understand reproaches such as the following: 'The fact that the intelligence is ill at ease in Christianity, and has been so for twenty centuries, comes from the failure to establish a satisfactory *modus vivendi* based on an exact understanding of the analogies and differences between the Holy Spirit speaking to the body of the Church and the Holy Spirit speaking to the soul' (*Connaissance Surnaturelle*, page 25). Simone was referring to a book she had been reading on Meister Eckart.

The supposed uneasiness of the intelligence is that of a mind which wants to construct ideas and systems, not of one which contemplates the reality revealed by God.

We can smile moreover at her objection to the anathemas when one reads the following sentence: 'A sacrament received unworthily does harm to soul and body' (*Connaissance Surnaturelle*, page 323). If it is so harmful as that, the Church which refuses it to the unworthy is acting in a motherly fashion!

The second thing which I said we have to bear in mind, but upon which I do not think it necessary to dwell, is the fact that Simone is all the more severe where her sympathy is engaged. For her, severity is a kind of sincerity, which would be admirable if regulated by truth and objectivity.

It must always be remembered that the only Church which attracts Simone Weil is 'the one in which Mass is celebrated' and that her attacks – reinforced by the writings of d'Aubigny which formed part of her favourite reading at Marseilles – never made her hesitate, so completely was she won over by the Eucharistic Presence, the mystics and the liturgy.

Her position would, moreover, be difficult to define; she used to say herself 'that it would need a book'. Such a definition would require a very exact knowledge of her vocabulary and her philosophic ideas. Simone proclaims her belief in the Christian faith, the reality of the mysteries and the supernatural life which she draws at its very source in the Church; but at the same time she does not wish to submit her intelligence to any authority – even though it be exercised in the name of God – which presents these truths, condemning error and indicating the necessary conditions for approaching the fount of grace. Here are two quotations in which she explains herself on this subject, the first was written at the beginning of July 1942, that is to say a few weeks after her departure from Marseilles, the second in London during the winter 1942–3. '. . . Moreover I cannot put the endorsement "*tala*" after my signature. I should not be allowed to do that, because I am not baptized, and yet it seem to me that in putting it I should not be lying. (There would be no lie, in any case, if the word be taken in its etymological sense.) I adhere completely to the mysteries of the Christian faith, with the kind of adherence which alone seems to me to be suitable for mysteries; this adherence is made of love, not assertion. Certainly, I belong to Christ; at least I like to think so.

'But I am kept outside the Church by difficulties of a philosophical order which I fear are insurmountable. They do not concern the mysteries themselves but the specifications with which the Church has thought good to surround them in the course of centuries, and, above all, the use in this connection of the words *anathema sit*.

'Although outside the Church, or more exactly on the threshold, I cannot help having a feeling that all the same I am really inside. Nothing is nearer to me than those who are inside.

'This is a spiritual position which is difficult to define or to make people understand. It would require pages and pages – or a book – but I must limit myself at present to these few words' (to M. Schumann).

'Wrongly or rightly, I do not think that I am outside the Church seen as a source of sacramental life, but only outside the Church as a social reality.' She had just said: 'Never should I blame those who are inside the Church; I should rather be inclined to envy them' (also to M. Schumann).

She believed she was meant to stay outside the Church, 'except perhaps at the moment of death' (Letter IV). Who will not feel the conflict and contradiction of such a position? It was a conflict which could only be resolved in the light of Christ who instituted his Church not to make friendship with him more difficult but to give us security in this friendship.

VI.

SYNCRETISM AND
CATHOLICITY

Simone Weil's discovery of the mystical value of prayer, sacraments and dogmas lessened her aversion for the Church and reduced it to a fear of the collective 'us'. In another direction it would appear that the conflict had merely been aggravated.

She must have already known – for she had been told and I had occasion to remind her of it – that the Church has never considered as lost those who through no fault of their own remain outside its visible fold. I had explained to her at great length Saint Thomas's doctrine concerning implicit faith (we know how she utilized this teaching and I will return to the subject later), but, immediately after her great illumination, she was so full of wonder at finding the expression of religious sentiment in non-Christian writings and, before even reading the works of the mystics of the Church, she had developed so pronounced a taste for the poetic and spiritual values of those races which had disappeared or fallen under oppression, that her mind remained set in that direction. In her London notes, she still sought to identify the angels with the gods of mythology and with the forces of matter. This is just one example among many, but it suggests the persistence of this tendency in her.

The question, however, is an historical one. It is not determined by personal ideas and dreams but by facts, evidences and documents. The history of religions and the interpretation of symbols and legends are not discovered by sudden poetic or spiritual intuitions.

She had such a gift for inventing likenesses without taking into account either places or dates, and of elaborating hypotheses while evading all the data which interfered with them that it was quite disconcerting at times.

For my part, I am inclined to think that a lack of historical objectivity, with all that this implies, was her mind's greatest lacuna. She would make sweeping statements without giving a thought to the inadequacy of her documentation: 'Saint Thomas is not Christian' . . . 'the Christians have never spoken of the spiritual value of virginity!' . . . *The Letter to a Priest*, in which she has summed up the reasons which kept her back from Catholicism, is a series of 'perhaps', 'doubtless' and assertions and difficulties depending on 'a tissue of suppositions'.

If time and years had been granted her, would she have consented to resume her constructive thinking in an objective way? Here we have the centre of her spiritual problem. It is necessary to try to understand her method, or rather her mind, in order to see the nature of the difficulties she had in matters of history, or better perhaps in matters touching on history.

Simone had poetic gifts of the very highest order and she was therefore extraordinarily sensitive to the prestige of words and images; she never hesitated over an association which she found poetically or spiritually felicitous or stimulating. Her method consisted entirely of 'attention', as she called it, and consequently depended on no objective checking. 'Method for understanding images, symbols, etc. Not to try to interpret them, but to look at them till the light suddenly dawns' (*Gravity and Grace*, 'Attention and Will', page 109). Is not this to be too oblivious of the fact that no human utterance can be rightly understood apart from its context in time and space? Apart from the person who utters it and the person to whom it is addressed? No doubt the words of God and even works of genius are not bounded by their period, nor perhaps by the minds which conceive them. All the same, this method is not suitable for history. A sentence such as 'It is necessary to have done with all the superstition of chronology in order to find eternity' (*Letter to a Priest*) may be dull of significance on the spiritual plane, but it is likely to introduce every kind of fantasy on the scientific plane of history. Simone connects the testimony of John, present on Calvary, with an esoteric Thibetan doctrine! She compares the baptistry, on account of its shape, with the ritual basin of antiquity and even with the sea itself. She links together Dionysus, Noah and Melchisedech because of the vine . . . we might make a long list of these associations of words or names. Was she always convinced by this mental sport? She comments thus on one of her theories in the article on the *Iliad*: 'Of course, this is mere fancy; one can see such distant times only in fancy's light' (*The Wind and the Rain*, vi, 4, page 244).

Her intimate friends had the impression once or twice, however, that she took herself in by this sport. The case of 'The Sons of Noah' is fairly typical. The idea of this article amused her and she confided it in a light-hearted, joking way to some of her close friends at Marseilles. Then, little by little, she fixed upon it and made it the centre of crystallization for a whole system of facts and ideas. Whoever studies this article with his heart will admire the elevation of soul and the spiritual beauty which breathe through it, but he who studies it with his reason, as a historian of religions, will discover a thousand absurdities in it; if Noah while he sleeps prefigures Christ, why does he no longer do so when he blesses his sons? If the religious destiny of humanity is not entrusted to this race, what is the whole story but a trivial family scene?

Those of Simone's friends who were historians have pointed out more than one partiality of this kind. One of them told me of this quaint incident: – Simone: 'But Herodotus said that . . . ' – The other speaker: 'It is necessary to criticize this testimony, by discovering its sources and meaning.' – Simone, outraged: 'Why should you want to criticize Herodotus?' – 'Why! because he is subject to criticism!'

With her desire for truth and her determination to preserve the individuality of her mind, she mistrusted all commentaries and notes. Thus she persisted in seeing in the admirable formula 'to do the truth', not a Hebrew saying but an Egyptian formula brought back by the Holy Family. That appears in the *Letter to a Priest*, with the note 'to be checked'. It is an example taken from among many. To choose to remain one's own teacher is to lay oneself open to many setbacks; the great masters – the true masters – are those who have put themselves to school under God and under men.

From time to time this spiritual method opens the way to intuitions which are so beautiful and so profound that one is amazed.

I recall two examples: 'Snow White who eats a little of one dwarf's bread, drinks a little from the glass of another and so on – this suggests the infinite consideration of the divine Presence which only makes itself felt in an infinitesimal manner' (unpublished fragment). This other fragment comes from the *Letter to a Priest*. It concerns the *Dies Irae*, a sequence of the fifteenth century: 'The idea of God going in quest of man is something unfathomably beautiful and profound. Decadence is shown as soon as it is replaced by the idea of man going in quest of God' (No. 34).

It is always good for us to be delivered from a childish interpretation of history. Divine values are entrusted to human frailty and for that reason are exposed to the empire of force; they have no connection, as far as we can see, with historical events. There was no successor to the greatest of bishops in the see of Hippo; the death and defeat of Saint Louis are of greater value than the most brilliant victories. The story of the invincible Armada should be conclusive in this matter: 'To illustrate this discussion and what we have said about the transcendence of the spiritual, let us think for a moment about the history of the invincible Armada. A most Catholic king, the whole of Spain praying, God's cause to be defended and promoted in the world, the centre of heresy to be crushed; was not another Lepanto a certainty? Just a little wind on the waters and the whole fleet is at the bottom. It is the reply of God himself. If we believe as we should in divine governance, we must conclude that God, who in the ordering of history has as the first end in view his Kingdom and his saints, here dissociated in a striking manner the interests of his glory and those of the forces who thought to save him. Doubtless the merits of the Tyburn martyrs – and future repercussions at which we cannot even guess – were of greater importance in the divine plan than the triumph of the Catholic king' (J. Maritain, *Religion et Culture*).

We spoke fairly often of this and we had no difficulty in agreeing about it: God's point of view is of the order of charity and cannot be measured in terms of military victories, election successes or even the life of nations. But, in order to establish her system, Simone was obliged, at any rate on some points, to form a conception of things which led her into historical difficulties and conflicted with the Christian conceptions. These difficulties were both the cause and the expression of her spiritual position with regard to Catholicism. We must insist a little upon this. Certain thinkers who are opposed to the idea of revelation, notably those who stem from Plato or Spinoza, conceive of all religions as good because they come from man and express his deepest needs and emotions. This is indifferentism. It is coherent in its negation. . . .

Simone rejected it because of her inner experience and the evidence which for her constituted revelation, yet she was unwilling to accept that the Christian vision of the universe was a grace from God. She therefore had to construct a system of her own of which the main points were that all religious traditions originated in revelation, that the message was transmitted in legend or folklore, that we have to trace equivalences in all the different cults and teachings – in short, a syncretism founded on the revelation of God himself.

It would take too long to follow in detail all the strange ideas to which this theory gave rise when it came to the spiritual interpretation of the legends of the different countries, and there is no doubt that Simone, had she published anything on this subject, would have revised more than one of the hasty intuitions which she had dashed off haphazard in a first rough draft and had never looked at again. At the same time it has to be recognized that it is here that her difficulties on Israel, on the Church and on Catharism are rooted.

At the centre of all her oppositions was her attitude to Israel, it was the key to all her resistance. Surely we have here a self-accusatory complex, a tendency to depreciate all that touched her nearly. Added to her other ideas was her dislike both for progress, which discriminates against all that comes before, and for privilege, which destroys equality. Her hostility towards Israel must indeed have been violent for the word 'fugitive slaves' to be used by her in a pejorative sense in this one and only connection!

She sees in the Gospel and the Incarnation the blossoming of the Greek genius. She says so in two texts which she had prepared for publication and which are worth quoting: 'Thus after three centuries of aridity, the spring of perfect purity welled up amongst the burning thirst of so many nations. The idea of mediation reached the fruition of reality, the perfect bridge appeared, divine wisdom became visible to the eye as Plato had longed that it should. The Greek vocation thus found its perfection by becoming the Christian vocation' (*L'Inspiration Occitanienne*, page 152). 'The Gospels are the last marvellous expression of the Greek genius, as the *Iliad* is the first; here the Greek spirit reveals itself not only in the injunction given mankind to seek above all other goods "the Kingdom and justice of our Heavenly Father", but also in the fact that human suffering is laid bare, and we see it in a being who at once is divine and human' ('The *Iliad*', *The Wind and the Rain*, page 245).

She is right in saying that Christ is the completion and crown of all things, and that all fullness dwells in him; but why does she forget that Our Lord chose to be a Jew to the very fringe of his garment and to the very manner of his discussions, parables and arguments? If she had had some regard for her historical data, if she had deepened her intuitions and made them universal, Simone could have shown most conclusively that Christ is the centre, the heir and the crown of all things. But by imagining this fraud which was supposed to have substituted Israel for Greece or Egypt as the forerunner and herald of Christ, she was throwing herself into a hopeless adventure. We will return to this.

As regards the Old Testament, she would never give up her point that the title 'God of Hosts', 'Yaweh Sabaoth', was impious and placed the Jewish religion below the pagan cults. Opposed to all Hebrew influences, she refused to see anything but war and massacre in them. I must own to having been surprised and somewhat amused at finding in her article on the *Iliad* a sentence like this: 'It is always they [the gods] who provoke those fits of madness, those treacheries, which are forever blocking peace; war is their true business; their only motives caprice and malice' (*The Wind and the Rain*, page 244). And in another place: 'They are set upon the destruction of men – the destruction of those who have been appointed by Zeus to suffer in grievous wars from youth to old age, until they perish to the last man' (*Iliad*, page 551; cf. *The Wind and the Rain*, page 237).

Why does Simone forget that the revelation of God and of creation was vouchsafed to Israel? That it was given to Moses to formulate the Great Commandment? Why does she pass over in silence the fact that the Old Testament was unique in forbidding human sacrifices? Why does she not quote the admirable injunctions concerning pity for the stranger, the needy . . . even to the goat which must not be cooked in its mother's milk?

Massacres and wars are among the scourges of humanity, they are not the unhappy privilege of antiquity. As for nations other than Israel, it is certain that they had great lights; a religious soul can gain much by meditating upon them. We used to dream of gathering together these inspired thoughts and combining them with the most beautiful Christian writings. It was for a work of this kind that she so longed to have the time: 'If you could arrange things so that we could have time to talk at our leisure of that choice of texts it would be a good thing' (Letter III).

The other great difficulty which the syncretic system of Simone Weil came up against was the conflict between Christianity at its birth and the pagan world. If there was equivalence or identity, why should they have disagreed instead of recognizing and embracing one another? The thousands of martyrs of the first centuries bore witness against idolatry and against any possibility of syncretism. Simone felt the truth of this and she therefore always tended to depreciate the martyrs. In order to understand their mentality, she compared them to those who had suffered similarly in revolutionary movements: their religious sentiment appeared to her to be impure: 'The God from whom the martyrs drew joy in torture or death is close to him who was officially adopted by the Empire and afterwards imposed by means of extermination' (*Gravity and Grace*, 'Affliction', page 76). Or else she represented divine beatitude as a created reward. 'In Corneille's *Polyeucte*: "But already in heaven the palm is waiting." A dog that jumps in order to be given a lump of sugar' (*Connaissance Surnaturelle*, page 310).

She used to say: 'The thought of death calls, for a counterweight, and this counterweight – apart from grace – cannot be anything but a lie' (*Gravity and Grace*, 'Imagination which Fills the Void', page 16). In order to know how the Christian martyrs really felt it is not necessary to invent theories, beautiful or otherwise, but to consult the documents, such as the letters of Saint Ignatius or of Saint

Cyprian and above all the 'Acts' of the martyrs, those official records in which their declarations were written down.

Moreover, some of the first Christians thought out and wrote about their Christianity, comparing it to the cults and philosophies of their contemporaries. I often urged Simone to study their writings. She had to postpone doing so on account of practical difficulties. Alas! when she spoke of the subject some months later, she could see nothing but inanities in Clement of Alexandria and imagined circumstances to nullify the testimony of this initiate of the Eleusinian mysteries.

In the case of Saint Justin, her gift for evading difficulties went further still: Justin sought God, he studied all the philosophies of his time (second century): Platonism, Stoicism, etc. An old man introduced him to the writings of the prophets and through them to Christ. Later he died a martyr under the Stoic Marcus Aurelius. His witness was therefore total and complete. Simone, however, was not in the least embarrassed. She decided that the prophecies through which the old man brought Justin to Christ, and which Justin himself used in his dialogue with the Rabbi Tryphon in order to prove Christ to be the Messiah, were too ancient and too beautiful to be from Israel. So, violating the text, she attributed them to Ham! (see *Connaissance Surnaturelle*, page 240). It would be out of place to insist too much upon this, since Simone never prepared the text for publication: it is a rough copy snatched from her by death and published without her consent. But it shows how she reacted; here was a fact which upset all her theories: she did not even dream of discussing who the old man really was. Since it was his advice to abandon Plato, he could not have been a Christian; since he praised the prophecies so much for leading to Christ, they could not have been the prophecies of Israel, in spite of the overwhelming evidence of the text. And then, making everything fit in by means of a wide and ill-digested erudition: the prophecies of Ham![1]

The same idea had been worrying her a few months earlier. She wrote to X: 'Of course all this is a tissue of suppositions, but one thing is practically certain, namely that they wanted to hide something from us and they have succeeded. . . . There has probably been a systematic destruction of documents' (*Letter to a Priest*, No. 35).

Taking all this into account, how is it possible, in the case of an unpublished rough draft, to speak of history or objectivity? Can one even speak of sincerity?

As for Catharism, building on the same insufficiency of information, she saw in the Albigensian movement a renaissance of the Greek spirit: 'The Greek spirit was reborn in the Christian form which is its truth' (*L'Inspiration Occitanienne*, page 152). So, of course, the Church of the thirteenth century was lamentably misguided. It is useless to prolong these remarks. Simone Weil might perhaps have come to realize for herself the fragility of her construction.[2]

Why did she fling herself into this adventure and allow herself to be carried away by such prejudices, such insufficient information and such unverifiable hypotheses? Mainly for two reasons: her love for those in affliction, whom she was anxious not to deprive of the presence of Christ: 'Christ is present on this earth wherever there is crime or affliction unless men drive him away. Otherwise what would be the meaning of the mercy of God?' (*Connaissance Surnaturelle*, page 36).

The other reason was her desire to integrate the secular life of the various peoples with Christianity: 'Humanism was not wrong in thinking that truth, beauty, equality are of infinite worth, but in thinking that man can obtain them for himself without grace' (*Inspiration Occitanienne*, page 158).

Struck by the spiritual impoverishment of the modern world, it was her dream to return to the sources, and above all to that pre-Christian religious inspiration which she supposed to be the soul of secular life. This was one of the reasons for her love of the twelfth century, in which Romanesque architecture and the troubadours flourished side by side with the Catharist puritans but independently of them: 'Whence will renewal come to us – to us 'who have defiled and emptied the whole earthly globe? From the past alone, if we love it' (*Gravity and Grace*, 'Social Harmony', page 155).

Simone devised this formula to which any child of the Church can assent: 'It is not a question of a Christian point of view and others, but truth and error. Not: what is not Christian is untrue, but everything that is true is Christian' (*Connaissance Surnaturelle*, page 24). The Christian knows that there is the truth which is offered to human discovery and the truth which God reveals to him, and that, moreover, there is no possibility of a conflict between them.

These views, in so far as they are justifiable, find their place in the Catholic synthesis: the Incarnation of Christ took place at a particular moment in history and yet it is 'the light which enlighteneth every man that cometh into the world' (John i. 9). The early Fathers insisted that certain preparations for Christianity were to be found in paganism; Saint Paul, standing before the Areopagus, based his appeal upon the cult of the Unknown God and the testimony of the poets. All medieval thought regarded the Sibylline books as being animated by the spirit of prophecy, Saint Thomas speaks of the Incarnation as being revealed to many pagans. The Church has always taught that Christ is the only Saviour and that no one, wherever he may be placed in space or time, can be saved without him; but it also teaches that his light enlightens every man, even if that man has never heard his name, and that thus all grace and truth come from him alone. Theology has ceaselessly declared that God is bound to give every being the means necessary to attain salvation and that there is no miracle he would not perform rather than allow anyone to be lost otherwise than by his own fault. Pius IX solemnly proclaimed this truth.

Theologians have recognized invisible means of grace outside the visible enclosure of the Church: the light of conscience, the partial truth preserved in false religions, the action of grace on particular persons, and miraculous interventions. It is moreover certain that the attitude of these theologians has varied according to the time at which they lived and their knowledge of non-Christian humanity. Certain currents of thought, especially at the present day, seek to find a sympathetic way of approach towards dissident Christians and towards non-Christian civilizations. This is not due to opportunism, but to an anxiety not to erect any barrier between the human race and its Saviour. The acceptance of veneration for ancestors, the consecration of native bishops, the choice of cardinals from among the coloured races and the introduction into the liturgy of artistic values from all civilizations show how far-reaching and profound is this movement. Indeed, it is the universal putting into practice of St. Paul's injunction to be all things to all men – a Jew among the Jews and a Gentile among the Gentiles – not out of opportunism but in order to gain all for Christ.[3]

It is in this perspective that, with its tentative approach and fundamental orientation, we have to understand the following fragment by Simone which I found recently: 'I must say that I have the same attitude of mind [attention] with regard to the other religions or metaphysical traditions and the other sacred writings, although the Catholic faith seems to me the most full of light. From the time of our first interviews I explained to you my difficulties concerning the other religions. You told me that no doubt with time these difficulties would lose their importance in my eyes. Truth compels me to say that, on the contrary, the more I think about it the more I feel the traditional attitude of the Church to be unacceptable. Also, the more I think about it, the more important I feel this point to be, for I think that the traditional attitude of the Church lowers not only the other religions but the Catholic religion itself. Yet now this no longer seems to constitute an insurmountable obstacle in the way of baptism. I think, perhaps wrongly, that the attitude of the Church on this point is not essential to the Catholic faith, and that the Church can change its attitude with regard to this as it has done with regard to astronomy, physics, biology and with regard to history and criticism. It even seems to me that it ought to change its attitude, that it cannot help doing so.

'I could say a great deal to you on this subject, but one has to limit oneself. I will just add this. Scripture itself gives clear proof, it seems to me, that long before Christ, at the very dawn of prehistoric times, there was a revelation greater than that made to Israel. I do not see what other interpretation could be given to the story of Melchisedech and to Saint Paul's commentary upon it. To read the passage of Saint Paul one might almost think it was a question of another incarnation of the Word. But, without going so far as that, the sentence: 'Thou are a priest for ever after the order of Melchisedech' shows conclusively that Melchisedech was connected with a revelation related to the Christian revelation, less complete, perhaps, but of the same level; whilst the revelation to Israel was of a very inferior level' (unpublished fragment).

What Simone here calls the 'traditional attitude' is based on what she thought she knew about it, chiefly from the Calvinistic or Jansenistic texts which she had read a great deal. She appeared to be surprised when she heard me quote the writings of Saint Thomas and of Pius IX; I found out afterwards that others had told her the same. Would she at length have understood the wisdom which proclaims the necessity for grace, connects all grace with Christ, but at the same time respects every human value which is capable of receiving or expressing this grace?

Furthermore, syncretism does away with universality, since it destroys unity and makes for a confusion in which nothing has any meaning, in which God is the author of the most extravagant and conflicting teachings. Catholicity, on the contrary, brings out both the universality of redemptive Love and the transcendent and marvellous unity to which all are called and in which all are hallowed and made one; the institution which it has founded is capable of becoming the city of God, stretching as wide as the universe.

To be fair, we should have to put all Simone Weil's texts side by side and to correct any rough notes she left by those which she had revised more carefully. We should see no doubt that her erudition and her information are very deficient in many points. The resemblances which she traces between Greece and Egypt belong to the decadent period and she is content to base her admiration of the whole of the Egyptian religion solely on the 'Book of the Dead'. Her intention is very clear, however: 'All these parallels, unless we were to deny the historical character of the Gospels, and this seems difficult if we are sincere, do not endanger the faith but are on the contrary an amazing confirmation of it. They are even necessary. We see everywhere – the lives of the Saints show it with remarkable clearness – that God has chosen to bind himself with regard to us in such a way that even his goodness depends on our prayer for its exercise. He can give us infinitely more than we can ask, for at the moment when we ask we do not yet know the fullness of good contained in what we ask. But, after the first attractions of grace, he does not give unless we ask. How should God have given his only

Son to the world if the world had not asked for him? This dialogue makes history infinitely more beautiful. In making people aware of it one could give human intelligence today the shock which it needs in order to bring a new attention to bear on the Christian faith.

'If one said to them: "That which produced the marvellous civilization of antiquity – with its art which we admire from so great a distance, with the science which it created entirely and which we have inherited, with its conception of the city which provides the framework for all our opinions, and with all the rest – that which produced all this was the age-long thirst for the spring which finally welled up and towards which today you do not even turn your eyes. . . ."' (*Intuitions Pré-Chrétiennes*).

'A historical incident of which the central character is God cannot but be refracted into eternity. Pascal speaks of "Jesus in agony until the end of the world", Saint John, with the supreme authority of the revealed texts, says that he has been slain since the foundation of the world. As, among the resemblances between the story of Prometheus and that of Christ, there is not one which is in the nature of an incident, they cannot in any way serve as an argument against the historical character of the Gospels. It follows that they only confirm and do not weaken dogma. Why, therefore, should anyone refuse to recognize them when they are self-evident?

'Apart from the New Testament itself and from the liturgy of Holy Week, nowhere could anything so poignant be found as certain passages of this tragedy expressing the love God bears us and the suffering united to this love.

'Is it not an extremely forcible thing to be able to say to all unbelievers: "without the overshadowing of the Passion, this Greek civilization, from which you draw all your thoughts without exception, would never have developed"' (*Intuitions Pré-Chrétiennes*).

'There are all sorts of arguments against such a conception of history, but as soon as one has adopted it, it appears so startlingly true that one is no longer able to abandon it' (ibid.).

Yet, once again, this work had only been roughly drafted; the historical foundations were too fragile, but how is it possible to judge the spiritual evolution of Simone Weil without reference to the deep purpose she here mentions?

Finally – Catholic in truth but not in fact. This more or less familiar notion provided Simone with one more pretext for remaining outside the Church. But did she understand that Catholicism is not a ready-made achievement? It is a call and a welcome. If the Church really is incomplete in any way (which is impossible when we see it as 'Jesus Christ shed abroad and communicated', but which is true when we consider it as the company of saints – a body which is in process of formation); if we are aware of this incompleteness, far from keeping away we should hasten our steps. No mission can be fully realized outside, for, even if we have had a glimpse of this mission before entering, its fruition is found in the service and enrichment of the Church.

Notes

[1] The foundation of this hypothesis is the quotation of an allusion made to Ham's prophecies by a gnostic of whom clement of Alexandria makes mention (cf. *Letter to a Priest*, No. 18). But even if they did exist, they have nothing to do with the case in point. Moreover, had she ever read Saint Justin, or only an article about him?

[2] A great deal has been said about her Catharism; a letter from her, said to have been written in 1940, was brought to light in 1947. In it she spoke of her admiration for the Catharist movement and used the word adherence as opposed to curiosity. . . .

If this letter really was written in 1940, I should say that in 1942 she had greatly changed and had no longer any traces of this attitude about her except her love of the twelfth century, where Romanesque architecture, the troubadours and the language and civilization of Provence (the *Pays d'Oc*) all shared her admiration. She wrote two articles about this in 1941–2 which appeared the following year in the *Cahiers du Sud*.

Simone had not taken time to study the doctrine of the Catharists, their organization and their methods of propaganda, but imagined them rather as a religious society without laws, holding a faith without dogma. She saw them as the negation of the Old Testament and as the heirs of the tradition of antiquity now harmoniously fused into a Christian philosophy. With all that, she thought of them as tolerant and humanistic, and began to love them without taking the trouble to know them in their historical reality. She based all this on a single piece of reading and she did not attempt to hide from me the slightness of her documentation. She thought, however, that we have to go back to the past in order to rediscover the source of inspiration. . . .

Moreover, all the texts in *Waiting on God* and the different unpublished writings from America and England to which I refer, came afterwards. I await the energetic controversialist who will convince me that when she was at Marseilles she had been initiated into the Eleusinian mysteries.

3   In this matter, the recent Encyclical of Pius XII is the best refutation of Simone Weil's ill-founded attacks. Here are some extracts: A quotation from the Epistle to Diognetus brings us back to the first centuries of the Church: 'Christians inhabit particular countries, but as sojourners; every foreign land is for them a home and their home-land is always a foreign country.'

Then come some definite assertions such as the following: 'The Church, from its origin until now, has always kept to the very wise rule by which the Gospel neither destroys nor stifles anything that is good, sincere and beautiful in the character and genius of the peoples which embrace it. . . . '

Another passage repeats the very words of the first Encyclicals of Pius XII: 'Innumerable researches and investigations, carried out in a spirit of sacrifice, devotion and love by the missionaries of all times, have sought to facilitate an intimate and respectful understanding of the most varied civilizations, and to make their spiritual values fruitful through a living and life-giving preaching of the Gospel of Christ. Everything in their customs and practices which is not indissolubly linked with religious error will always be sympathetically examined and whenever possible protected and encouraged. . . . '

VII.

PERSONAL PROBLEMS

Simone has described with exceptional depth and intensity those conflicts in which she was torn between the mystical and the social, the supernatural and the human. They were enhanced by the grace which called and enlightened her, the formation of her mind with its habit of attention for all it touched, and finally by her experience which was perhaps unique and gave her an inside knowledge both of the most cultivated intellectual circles and of working-class and revolutionary movements in full effervescence. Yet one might say that such conflicts are not unusual and are a reflection of the age in which we are living.

How would she finally have resolved them? By a living experience of the Catholic synthesis which is at the same time intimate and universal? Or would she have worked out a wisdom of her own, as opposed to all others, a personal gnosis? Who can say? For my own part, having known her as I did, I am still inclined to think that, in spite of all the difficul-ties she encountered and would have had to encounter, she would have ended by attaining to the total vision of light, and I still place her soul above her genius. When I say this I am not denying the personal difficulties she had in her religious search; I think that the obstacles were more numerous and her conflicts went deeper in this region than in that of ideas, but there was a generosity in her and a will to be faithful which, according to the divine promise, cannot fail to reach the light. It is of this aspect that I want to speak now, without attempting, for all that, to embark upon a psychological study of Simone Weil – which is not in the least in my line. It would be possible to make a long list of the inner conflicts which were at the root of her acute sense of incompleteness: the desire for loyalty contrasting with non-objectivity, humility with aggressiveness, a conscious taste for mimesis with a refusal to bind herself, accessibility with a defensive complex, disgust at self with assertiveness, a sense of her own wretchedness with universal severity. . . . I will confine myself to a few more important characteristics which help in the understanding of her religious difficulties.

The first personal problem, which had to do with the form of her mind and her philosophic ideas – ideas, moreover, which were not peculiar to her but are shared by all the modern world – was that of intelligence itself. She wrote to me: 'The intelligence is a specifically and rigorously individual thing' (Letter IV, *Waiting on God*, page 29). Thus she considered the intelligence to be more linked to the individual subject than to the object which is the same for all. Driven by her sense of affliction and by the supernatural significance which she discovered in the power of compassion, she came to wish (and this as a summit): 'That animal sensitivity even should become universal; that is contradictory, miraculous, supernatural' (*Connaissance Surnaturelle*, page 71). She had not yet discovered that this universal range is the property of the intelligence more than any faculty, and that the intelligence should indeed have this quality. How was it to attain to the central truth, that truth which should be within the reach of each one of us at every moment and which should be communicable to all others, without becoming universal itself (itself above all), and in consequence impersonal – supra-personal? She glimpsed this truth at times and thus she wrote: 'The subjective theories of knowledge are a perfectly correct description of the state of those who do not possess that very rare quality of coming out of themselves' (*Connaissance Surnaturelle*, page 335); she only saw it however as a 'supernatural faculty', 'charity', which was, moreover, independent of the sacrament of baptism.

Grace had given her the power to come out of herself, but she struggled with this conflict except in the realm of what she called 'contact with the transcendent'.

This passive method, of opening to inspiration, this attention, as she herself called it, can only be of value when it is preceded by a fairly comprehensive study of the sources and data of a problem and an objective examination of it. I recall the American inventor's receipt for genius – a somewhat heavy paraphrase of the old definition: 'a long patience':[1] 'I can tell you what genius is made of: one percent of inspiration and ninety-nine percent of perspiration', a sentence which we might compare with the injunction of Saint Vincent de Paul: 'We have to love God in the sweat of our brow', not only by eagerly labouring in devoted service, but also by diligently applying ourselves to the religious quest.

Simone was still lacking in knowledge of Catholicism, of the Christian texts and sources, of the thought of the Church and even of Catholic realities. This accounts for many lacunæ in her intuitions, many unfounded reproaches and perhaps an insufficient effort to be completely objective.

This conflict between her love of truth and her attachment to her own ideas comes out very strikingly when we consider a passage such as the following: 'I must give you the impression of a Luciferian pride in speaking thus of a great many matters which are too high for me and about which I have no right to understand anything. It is not my fault. Ideas come and settle in my mind by mistake, then, realizing their mistake, they absolutely insist on coming out. I do not know where they come from, nor what they are worth, but, whatever the risk, I do not think I have the right to prevent this operation' (Letter IV, *Waiting on God*, page 32). This is her judgment of her own intelligence: unexpected ideas shone out in her mind, she did not exactly know where they came from; they were not the conscientious elaboration of a close study of all the facts of the problem, but were, rather, a flash of illumination. She did not pride herself on the discovery this brought, nor even claim that it had any value; she did not always make the necessary effort to test the truth of it; but, from a scrupulous fear of failing in fidelity, she felt it to be her duty to express these ideas. She made them known all the more readily and energetically if they went against her inclinations and her cherished tastes, finding in this very opposition a guarantee of their truth (her attacks on Israel and Christianity are often of such a nature). This confidence Simone had brings us to the heart of her conflict – a conflict which doubtless went all the deeper because she was an intellectual.

We have to remember it when we read her writings, and above all her notebooks. She felt it as a duty to record in them everything which came into her mind. Even in a letter which had been prepared with a rough copy and most carefully corrected, she owned that she did not know what her ideas were worth but that she was letting them come out at random.

This deep attraction she felt for the constructions of her mind, to which her poetic intuition, the width of her extensive culture, a scrupulous love of truth and an attachment to her own ideas and even to the free play of her fancy all contributed, is very characteristic of her thought. It led her to imagine an order of theoretic speculation in which authors would have the right to say anything, to affirm or deny anything without admitting any responsibility and without claiming to influence the thought of their readers! That she felt this as an essential need reveals the somewhat unrealistic and visionary side of her nature.

Hence, thanks to the vigour of her mind and the wealth of her culture, came her views of high spirituality and intuitions which were far-reaching and penetrating; but hence, also, the wild systematizations, the statements without enough facts to support them, the exaggerations and partialities, and a tendency to disregard the thousands of miles and the centuries dividing what she brought together – all the things, in fact, for which she is rightly criticized. But it must always be remembered that never in the course of her life did she publish anything concerning religious matters; if I myself had such hesitation in sanctioning the publication of certain texts – texts over which, moreover, she had pondered, since they had been put into order – it was precisely because I knew her scruples concerning intellectual honesty and the consciousness she always had of not having reached her full development.

It must, however, be observed that she attached a certain importance to some of her systematizations, since she based her opposition to Our Lord's words upon them; this is perhaps one of the weaknesses which show her intelligence to have been merely exposed to the flames and not 'cooked' – that is to say fundamentally transformed – by the Fire of the Spirit, to use one of Simone Weil's own beautiful comparisons.

To love God with all one's mind, as the Great Commandment enjoins, is to be open to the truth wherever it comes from, either from friend or foe; it is to be objective, to accept or withhold one's agreement according to the weight of the evidence. It is, above all, to listen to God and to allow his light to fashion, deepen and amplify our poor spirit by filling it with his Word.

This was a subject to which we often returned. From time to time, indeed, Simone would arrive with some new idea or unforeseen difficulty; then I would ask for her proofs, the texts on which she was basing her statement; I showed her the other points of view, the divine words which she had not taken into account and, avoiding any discussion which would have been useless, I left her to reflect. This method, of which the aim was to make her objective, to lead her not to impute to a text any meaning except that which it expressed, to take dates and environment into account, made a great impression on her but was not without difficulties. Hence some of her reproaches.

Her love of truth was also affected by her fear of being influenced. There is no denying that she was very permeable to the ideas and sentiments of the circles in which she moved; the statements in her letters with regard to this are not merely declarations of humility, as people say. She had therefore developed a strange defensive complex, a sensitive reserve which made her suspicious of all friendship. No doubt there was a scrupulous love of truth in this, but was there not exaggeration masking an attachment to her own ideas which obstructed the truth? Her aggressiveness made one fear this to be the case; it was a rather strange characteristic of her personality. In the case of B (Letter IV), she reproached me for not recognizing what she called his 'implicit faith'. Yet, not only was I able to see for myself when I made his acquaintance two or three years later that I had had good grounds for my reserve, but further, when some of Simone's letters to him were communicated to me, I found to my surprise that when writing to him she shared my point of view. This is only a detail but I think it too significant to be passed over in silence. As soon as we try to circumscribe a person in order to assess his personality, we discover that all our measures are too short.

It would be a long business to make a list of all that met with Simone's hostility or censure: the Jews came first, of course!

Then the Romans, the medieval Church, the people of northern France, the Corsicans, Aristotle, Saint Thomas, Maritain, etc.!

But it must be repeated that she was just as severe with herself; it must also be repeated that it was in the nature of her intelligence to react with all the more violence if she was opposing accepted ideas . . . or friendships.

These over-hasty reactions, with no withdrawal and with no time to verify the facts in all their bearings, often gave her words the one-sidedness of polemic or the vehemence of invective.

How many times when I was with her I heard within me the music of those ineffable words, 'I praise thee, O Father, Lord of heaven and earth, because thou hast revealed these things to little ones.'

Another characteristic which must not be forgotten was the sense, or one should rather say the crushing burden, of her wretchedness. It came from the physical pain which had been there within her since she was twelve 'surrounding the central point of her nervous system . . . so that all attempts at attention and intellectual work were as hopeless as those of a condemned man awaiting execution' (cf. Letter to Joë Bousquet).

In the rough copy of a letter she was preparing for me, she had written and then rubbed out 'after having suffered as you know I do'; later, when she was in London, she attributed to 'the crushing burden of physical pain' what she called 'her criminal error concerning pacifist groups' (*Connaissance Surnaturelle*, page 317).

Yet there was infinitely more than that in her. She wrote to G. Thibon: 'I shall never forget the generosity which made you say and write to me some of those things which warm and cheer us even when, as in my case, it is impossible to believe them' (Introduction to *Gravity and Grace*, page xiv), and she wrote in her note-books at the same period: 'It is not by chance that you [meaning herself] have never been loved' (*Gravity and Grace*, page 59). We remember with what moving gratitude she spoke of the months spent at Marseilles in her farewell letter.

This same consciousness of misery often weighed her down in her deeper life and erected a wall between her and the sacraments. It did not consist of formula, it was a reality of soul which the divine promises could not destroy. There is no doubt that we must attach

great importance to this avowal in the Prologue: 'I understood that
he had come to fetch me by mistake. . . . Sometimes I cannot help
repeating with fear and remorse a little of what he said to me. How
am I to know if I remember it accurately? He is not there to tell me.
I know quite well that he does not love me. How could anyone
love me? And yet at the bottom of my heart, something, a point
of myself, cannot help thinking while trembling with fear that
perhaps, after all, he does love me' (*Connaissance Surnaturelle*,
page 10).

She was obsessed with this unworthiness as soon as she began
to envisage the possibility of entering the Church. She spoke of it
repeatedly and her first letter of January 1942 alludes to it. Eight
or nine months later she spoke of it again to the American priest
(*Letter to a Priest*), and in the London notebook she returned to it.
'One might think that there are souls who are irremediably
ineligible for the service of God on account of the inadequacy of
their nature. I among them' (*Connaissance Surnaturelle*, page 380).
What a number of allusions there are in these notebooks to
this painful and poignant sense of her wretchedness! How many
times she brings home to us how great a burden action was for her!
But she realized the value of it: 'Disgust in all its forms is one of the
most precious trials sent to man as a ladder by which to rise. I have
a very large share of this favour. We have to turn all this disgust into
a disgust for ourselves' (*Gravity and Grace*, page 158).

In spite of her reserve she came back from time to time to
this suffering. Christian humility, however, should go beyond this
disgust in order to have done with the self and to open the way for
divine mercy – that mercy which goes so far as to forget our sins and
would have us rise above our wretchedness. But has this gift ever
been granted to a mortal being outside the Eucharistic communion?

We must also mention among the special problems of Simone
Weil her unyielding resolution not to allow her attention to rest on
any dogmas which might interfere with her will to achieve purity
or hinder her effort to go to God through unconsoled affliction:
'Everything can be turned to use. *Etiam peccata*. This is not to be
believed in too much, for it is a thought which cures bitterness and
fills up the void, like the belief in immortality or in the providential
ordering of events' (*Connaissance Surnaturelle*, page 113).

She already held this opinion at Marseilles: there are several traces of it in *Gravity and Grace*. It can be disputed, for Our Lord himself spoke of the greatness of his promises, and Saint Paul reminds us that there can be no possible comparison between the momentary sufferings of this world and the stupendous glory of eternity. But we have to beware of those human representations which are a caricature of Christian hope. We do not look for blessings of a human variety or a life of unlimited duration, but God himself – God becoming all in all and seen as he is – God gathering his children together and filling them with his divine life.

Another characteristic which we cannot pass over in silence was Simone's attempt to achieve impersonality by making herself more and more obedient to God. This was one of the ideas which dominated her spiritual personality and there is not a doubt but that it was one of the deepest causes of her inner conflict. She made an ideal of passivity or depersonalization, and took matter as a perfect example. One might sometimes think that she saw in it the very perfection of God: 'It is that [blind impartiality characteristic of inert matter] which is held up as a model of perfection to the human soul. It is a conception of so profound a significance that we are not even today capable of grasping it' (*The Need for Roots*, page 251). Indifference appears to her to be perfection.

Her philosophical culture, and particularly the influence of the Stoics and of Spinoza, had predisposed her to this and it was in this sense that she understood Christ's words concerning the goodness of the heavenly Father who gives the sunshine and rain to all alike.

In spite of all her assertions, and, still more, from the very fact of her own experience, I continue to think that there is a gulf between Stoic and Christian virtue, but I do not deny, all the same, that it is possible for some people to practise Stoicism in a Christian way. Considerable developments are possible as principles pass from theory to life. Some for the better, some the worse.

But Simone's temperament, so painfully and deeply marked with the consciousness of her unworthiness and limitations, was inclined to self-abasement, she tended to trample on her tastes, to go against herself, almost to reduce herself to nothing; thus her humility, real as it was, was still full of self and sometimes became a form under which her *ego* reappeared.

With such ideas, she became overwhelmingly convinced that obedience to God is the greatest of goods, that it must be placed above all others in time and eternity; this thought became an obsession with her. 'I have a terror of disobedience,' she wrote; and again, on the same subject: 'This unconditional "yes" which is spoken in the most secret part of the soul and which is only silence, is completely preserved from all danger of contact with force. Nothing else in the soul can be preserved from it. This method is simple, there is no other. It is the *amor fati*, the virtue of obedience, the most Christian of all virtues. But this "yes" is only of value when it is unconditional. The slightest mental reserve, almost unconscious, is enough to take from it all its effectiveness. If it is unconditional, it really transports the part of the soul that pronounces it to heaven, to the very bosom of the Father. It is as wings' (*Intuitions Pré-Chrétiennes*).

Scrupulosity, gnawing at this beautiful desire, led her to a contradiction. She thought she ought to do nothing on the plane of her relationship with God unless she had received a definite inspiration, an irresistible impulsion. 'There is only one case in which it is legitimate to talk about particular volition on the part of God: that is when a particular impulsion arises in a man's soul which bears the impress of God's commandments. But it is then a question of God considered as a source of inspiration' (*The Need for Roots*, page 271). Without such a personal command, the most solemn and universal declarations were not enough for her, and she thought she had to remain in a state of waiting – waiting to which both the consciousness of her imperfection and the thought of her mission (the two of them rather hard to reconcile together, incidentally) each in turn prompted her.

Moreover this method had succeeded with her. Was it not Our Lord himself who had taken the initiative in enlightening her when she was not searching for him, and in making known to her the splendour of prayer? She forgot that divine interventions are vouchsafed in order to attract our attention (the star of the Magi disappeared so that they should be obliged to consult the prophecies), or, at any rate, she did not apply this to herself. Her philosophy did not predispose her very much to understand the part played by intelligence and liberty in the religious quest.

Christ's words are clear and forceful enough to need no commentary. But Simone, who recognized this elsewhere, did not immediately see its application to herself. She felt that she was united with the mass of unbelievers, she believed herself to be entrusted with a mission which, according to her, must delay, perhaps until death, her entrance into the Church and her reception of the Body of the Lord.

One day when she was speaking to me of this and I was telling her about the life of some saint – I no longer remember which – I said: 'You want to attract others to Christianity without becoming a Christian yourself, so you want to be like the bell which calls people to the Church it does not enter.' Some have criticized me for having too much insisted on this incident; but they forget that it was Simone who, struck by the comparison, repeated the story to some friends who themselves published it.

It is worth dwelling on this conflict between her consciousness of a mission and her hesitations about engaging herself as a Christian. There may have been illusion there, but it is also possible that grace had given her a sense of such a duty even before she had completed her evolution; she would not have been the first to have this intuition before the light of faith shone in its full clarity; I have come across experiences of this kind on several occasions.

Face to face with Simone Weil I contented myself with reminding her of the definite injunctions of Our Lord and with insisting upon the absolute duty of detachment, which is the very foundation of the religious search and the abandonment of our views, our tastes and prejudices in order to give ourselves up to his action, not passively, but with absolute fidelity to what he shows us from day to day. 'Birds resort into their like; so truth will return to them that practise her' (Ecclesiasticus xxvii. 10). More forcibly still the Master says: 'He that doeth truth cometh to the light' (John iii. 21).

I think that all these conflicts between faithfulness to her own ideas and objectivity, between docility and personal discovery, between passivity and activity, between a sense of her wretchedness and joy in the divine mercy, like all the others, would have been resolved on the level of sanctity. There extremes are found reunited and there also is the intermediary; there the impersonal and the personal meet in the supra-personality of Christ living in his own. Simone guessed it; she had a clear idea of this ideal, but she was also conscious of the distance which still separated her from it.

Note

[1]   Cf. Carlyle's definition: 'An infinite capacity for taking pains.'

VIII.

THE LAST MONTHS

On 16th May 1942 Simone left Marseilles; we had known each other for less than a year; she told the friend to whom we owed our introduction of the joy it had brought her and the great progress she had made during the year in her discovery of the Church. The writings she sent me from Casablanca towards the end of May belong to the same period as our conversations – indeed, she had already started to write her farewell letter on the 14th (that is the date at the beginning of the first rough copy). What was the course of her development after that? It is difficult to say with any precision. To help us to follow it we have her writings and a few pieces of evidence which are too partial and incoherent to allow of a really objective judgment.

What value should we attach to the following testimony from one of her friends: she said to a sceptic, in order to obtain permission for one of his daughters to be baptized, that it did not bind one in any way and might be useful for the child if later on she wanted 'to marry a Catholic' [sic]. What does such a declaration mean? That Simone thought lightly of baptism? Or that, valuing it very highly, she wanted to do everything possible to gain permission for it and was hiding her real sentiments by using an argument which could not deceive anybody, particularly since this happened in a country where there is a Protestant majority.

What value should we attach to the testimony from London that, with regard to baptism, she repeated that she was 'waiting' and that this was definite enough to make one of her friends still regret that she did not herself baptise her?

Another friend told me that she seemed as though she was 'weary of her search'; and again another found Simone subtle, talkative and evasive – avoiding discussion.

When we come to her writings, what do we discover about her inner development? There is first of all, to my knowledge, the long *Letter to a Priest* where we again find her in conflict. What strikes me personally here is her subjectivism: 'When I read the catechism of the Council of Trent, it seems to me that I have nothing in common with the religion there set forth. . . . ' And yet a few months before, through the notes of a treatise (unfortunately I cannot be sure which of the chapters she read, some were only roughly sketched and some in order), she recognized herself as belonging to the Catholic faith presented as the revelation of God's love.[1]

Most important of all, the letter continues with these words which show the attraction she felt for the religion of the liturgy and the Eucharist: 'When I read the New Testament, the mystics, the liturgy and when I see Mass celebrated, I feel with a kind of certainty that this faith is mine, or, more exactly, would be mine if it were not for the distance which separates me from it because of my imperfections.'

Then we are taken right through the questions which held her back or could hold her back. She wanted to know exactly the judgment of the Church on these points. She came back to questions she had resolved, as for instance that of implicit faith which I had explained to her at length, supporting what I said by the actual words of Saint Thomas.[2]

L'Enracinement (*The Need for Roots*) contains invectives against the Church – we know the aspect of it which Simone designates under this name and I will not return to that. As to the ideas concerning Providence and miracles, it is to be wondered what her inward attitude was: was her philosophy stifling her previous conviction? Was she reacting against certain conceptions she had met with which were too puerile? Her thought was often a reaction. Should we insist on the physical and psychological conditions of her work? Or was she only expressing one aspect of her thought? Her favourite ideas are to be found here, the best and the worst; I have referred to them in several places. Personally, having seen her desire to open to the truth and the work of grace in her, I am inclined to interpret them in the most favourable light, but certain points of view are definitely unacceptable, certain judgments are flagrantly unjust. . . . Would she herself have published the book in this form?

And then, what is to be said about *La Connaissance Surnaturelle*? Should it not reveal her most intimate thoughts? So I myself had supposed. The hypothesis of a relapse can never be dismissed; most souls do not develop in accordance with the rules of abstract logic but rather by oscillations and sudden leaps forward. Simone knew this herself: 'It is very possible that after having passed weeks, months or years without thinking about it at all, one day I shall suddenly feel an irresistible impulse to ask immediately for baptism and I shall run to ask for it. For the action of grace in our hearts is secret and silent' (Letter I, *Waiting on God*, page 6).

Personally, I was not so much affected by her attacks on the Church, since I understood their very special meaning, nor by the arguments against the faith, nor by Simone's other intellectual faults; I knew them already and I do not think that there is anything really new here. What did disconcert me, however, was the reappearance of questions which she had considered as settled, of statements which she had seen to be false or unfounded and of criticisms without objectivity. I now think that the importance of all this must be reduced considerably, though in exactly what proportion is known only to God.[3]

In the first place it must be noticed that Simone confided far less to her notebooks than one would be inclined to expect. She wrote a great deal and even needed large-sized paper so that she could express herself freely by letting her thoughts flow . . . this was the same with her letters. Yet it seems as though she kept the great secrets of her deeper life in an inviolable silence. As far as I am able to know, she only spoke to Joë Bousquet and myself of the great light which changed her life; her most intimate companions had no suspicion of it and she confided it to none of her notebooks. It was the same at Saint-Marcel when she discovered the meaning of prayer: neither did G. Thibon, who had become her intimate friend, know anything about it, nor was there a hint of the experience in her voluminous notebooks.

We must not therefore exaggerate the importance of Simone Weil's notebooks. They consist mainly of rough drafts of her thoughts – and this brings us to another consideration.

Simone's usual method of working was to examine a question, not only when she thought it to be doubtful, but even when she knew it to be false. In order to discover the force of an affirmation, she immediately tried to find out what truth was contained in the opposite negation. How then are we to distinguish between a scaffolding which she intended to remove, the doubts of a moment, a first intuition, and the expression of her finally considered thought?

Moreover, side by side with mere jottings, quotations without references, and notes of what she had been reading, we come upon sentences of great value concerning the consciousness of her wretchedness and Christ as the model before whom we must efface ourselves: 'To take Christ for our model. Through attention, a true artist identifies himself with what he looks at. Meanwhile his hand moves and the paint brush with it. . . . That is the way in which Christ should be our model. We must think of Christ. Christ, not our image of Christ. We must think of Christ with our whole soul. Meanwhile the mind, will, etc., and the body are active. . . . To this end we must think of Christ as man and God' (*Connaissance Surnaturelle*, page 334).

There are also passages of real greatness where, even if she does not wish to consider the problem of immortality, we can see with what sincerity she approaches the solemn moment of death. But, yet again, this does not reveal her innermost thoughts and feelings with regard to the great problem.

All the same, in order to obtain permission to go on a dangerous mission, she allowed herself to make a truly precious confidence: 'Apart from what I might be permitted to do for the good of other human beings, life for me personally has no other meaning, and in reality never has had any other meaning, than a waiting for the revelation of truth.

'I am ceaselessly and increasingly torn, both in my intelligence and in the depth of my heart, through my inability to conceive simultaneously and in truth of the affliction of men, the perfection of God and the link between the two.

'I have an inward conviction that if the vision of this truth is ever vouchsafed to me it will only be when I myself am psychically in affliction, and in one of the extreme forms of the present affliction.

'I am afraid that this will not happen. Even when I was a child and thought that I was an atheist and a materialist, the fear was always present to me that I should fail, not over my life but over my death. This fear has never ceased to grow in intensity.

'An unbeliever might say that my desire is egotistical because the vision of truth, received at such a moment, can no longer be of any use to anyone.

'But a Christian cannot think in this way. A Christian knows that a single thought of love raised to God in truth, although mute and without an echo, is more useful, even for this world, than the most brilliant action.

'I am outside the truth, no human thing can transport me into it, and I have the inner certainty that God will transport me into it in no other way than that. It is a certainty of the same kind .as the certainty at the root of what men call a religious vocation.

'That is why I cannot help having the barefaced indiscretion and importunity of a beggar' (Letter to M. Schumann).

A little later she confided to the same friend what attitude is worthy of the divine favour: 'The slave who is to be loved is he who stands upright and motionless by the door in a state of watching, waiting, attention, desire – ready to open as soon as he hears a knock.

'Neither weariness, nor hunger, nor the requests, the friendly invitations, the blows or jeers of his companions, nor the rumours which may be circulated round him to the effect that his master is dead or angry and determined to hurt him – nothing will disturb in the slightest degree his attentive stillness.'

Be you 'like to men who wait for their Lord when he shall return from the wedding; that when he cometh and knocketh they may open to him immediately. Blessed are those servants whom the Lord when he cometh shall find watching. Amen I say to you that he will gird himself and make them sit down to meat and passing will minister unto them.'

The state of waiting, rewarded in such a way, is what is ordinarily called patience. But the Greek word ὑπομονῆ is infinitely more beautiful and bears a somewhat different meaning.

It suggests a man who waits without moving in spite of all the blows given to try to make him move.

καρποφο ροῦσιν ἐν ὑπομονῆ

'They will bring forth fruit in waiting.'

These sentences with which the confidential journal of London ends are without a doubt among the last words written by Simone Weil. In them she returns to ideas and even to formulæ which were dear to her and which she had dwelt on elsewhere, even at Marseilles the year before.

This was not the only time that she was pleased to number herself among the unprofitable servants who had used up their strength in labour and had no right to anything.

Was it given to her to understand that Christ wishes something infinitely better for his own and for those 'who believe in him through their word'? 'I will not now call you servants: for the servant knoweth not what his Lord doth' – and that is why he has to watch and wait – 'I have called you friends: because all things, whatsoever I have heard of my Father, I have made known unto you' (John xvi. 15).

Did Simone rediscover 'the attic' where the Lord confides his secrets? Did she come to understand that she had her place in it? Did she believe and give herself up to the secret instinct which assured her, in spite of herself, of the divine love? Did she find the faith in its fullness which the Church repeats to us means this confidence in the divine friendship?

Mystery surrounds the meeting of the soul with God.

Notes

[1] *Mystère de la Charité* (Office général du Livre).

[2] I will not repeat the terms quoted in *L'Eglise dans ma vie* in order to show the doctrine of the Church concerning the salvation of those who are outside the faith.

It is to be regretted that the publication without notes or indications and without answers of this text from America gives to something which was only the subject of discussions the character of something absolute. None of these difficulties really had a foundation; most of them came from an insufficiency of information or from the perpetual raising of objections which, had it not been for her defensive complex, would have been finally resolved at Marseilles.

The mystics and the liturgy show Catholicism fully lived; the Mass is the centre of the Church; it is there that she would have found herself to be at home when the irresistible attraction of the Eucharist had finally wrenched her free from the sense of her imperfection.

3   We must not forget that the Prologue was written at Marseilles and, if we are looking for exactitude in a poem, 'it was no longer winter, it was not yet spring', so we should date it in March or April. It does not, therefore, throw light on the American note-books, but on her discoveries at Marseilles; her fear not to have understood the divine revelation, the consciousness of her unworthiness and the hope of being loved in spite of everything.

IX.

SPIRITUAL SIGNIFICANCE

Is it possible to say what would have been the spiritual outcome of such a development had its earthly course not been cut short by Simone's premature death at the age of thirty-four?

Would she finally have resolved her conflicts and achieved unity in Christ's peace, that peace which triumphs over our anguish and brings contraries into harmony? Personally, as I have said, I am inclined to think so, because of the divine words: 'He that doth truth cometh to the light.' But by what roundabout ways? by what trials? For the Master also said: 'Unless you become as little children' – children not because of our ignorance but because of that simplicity which is compatible with the most consummate learning and the highest genius. Grace is given in abundance, but we have to reckon with man's free-will and with conditions of environment and temperament which tend to obstruct the light even without any personal fault.

What would Simone's spiritual development have been? I am aware of the upward force which raised her, or rather the force of attraction by which she admitted herself to be so irresistibly drawn that she saw in it a proof of God: it was the 'proof by perfection' (unpublished) – 'An ontological proof . . . If I am really raised up, this something is real' (*Gravity and Grace*, 'Contradiction', page 90). I am also aware, however, of all there was in her that resisted; intellectual difficulties and the formation of her mind; scrupulosity which created difficulties and exaggerated them. 'The action of truth awakens falsehood from its inertia and causes it to defend itself; that is the meaning of the temptation of the saints' (*Connaissance*

Surnaturelle). With a subtlety which leads one in spite of oneself to guess that she was speaking from experience, she has analysed at length the way the lower part of the soul reacts to the sacrament: 'All the mediocre part of the soul feels a repugnance for the sacrament, hates it and fears it much more than the flesh of an animal shrinks back in order to escape the death which is coming to it' . . . 'The more real the desire for God, and in consequence the contact with God through the sacrament, the more violent the revolt of the mediocre part of the soul; a revolt which can be compared with the shrinking back of living flesh which is about to be put in the fire. This, according to the different cases, has the predominant character of repugnance, hatred or fear. . . . In its desperate effort to survive and to escape destruction by fire, the lower part of the soul, with feverish activity, invents arguments. It borrows them from no matter what arsenal, including theology and all the warnings about the dangers of the unworthy reception of sacraments. So long as these thoughts are completely disregarded by the soul in which they arise, the inner tumult is infinitely blessed. The more violent the inward movement of drawing back, of revulsion and fear, the more is it certain that the sacrament is going to destroy a great deal of evil in the soul and to carry it much nearer to perfection.'

Which way was the victory to go? All Simone's culture, her philosophical training, her deep-seated tendencies, inclined her to form her own opinions; all the grace of Christ encourages docility to God in an attitude which is at once the most reasonable and the most suprarational possible.

What is certain is that, in spite of all her resistances, she was supernaturally attracted only to 'The Church in which Mass is celebrated' (cf. *Letter to a Priest*). A very evident sign of her deepest and most conscious intentions has not been sufficiently stressed. It is the fact that she chose as her spiritual legatees two people whom she knew to be attached to the Church with all their souls – G. Thibon and myself.

If we were to take beauty as the criterion of truth, we should have to conclude that the months at Marseilles, with 'The Love of God and Affliction', 'The Right Use of School Studies', 'Forms of the Implicit Love of God', and the 'Prologue'[1] showed the best orientation of her mind.

Without giving way to conjecture, which is always unwise, can we try to decipher something of this mysterious and uncompleted destiny? Simone sent me her autobiography with a definite intention: 'When I let you have a written sketch of my spiritual autobiography, I had a reason. I wanted to make it possible for you to see for yourself a concrete and certain example of implicit faith. Certain, for I know that you know that I am not lying. Wrongly or rightly you think that I have a right to the name of Christian' (Letter VI, *Waiting on God*, page 41).

Does the case of Simone Weil fit in with the Christian conception of the supernatural world or does it not? To avoid confusion I would make one preliminary observation: whatever she may have said to me about it, she was mistaken in using the expression 'implicit faith'. The implicit faith of which the theologians speak is an adherence which is conscious, as regards certain truths recognized by the reason, and implicit, as regards certain supernatural truths necessary to salvation, which the believer, who is a Christian without realizing it, holds to be true while still in ignorance of the fact; for instance, a person who believes in God as Providence and loves him with adoration although he has not even had the Gospel preached to him, is unconsciously included in the redemptive plan and receives all its riches. 'Without faith it is impossible to please God.' How could one be in charity, and thus on the way leading to salvation, without admitting, at least obscurely and implicitly, that God loved us and was inviting us to be his friends? With Simone the case was quite different; she knew the Christian doctrine, believed in God, the mystery of the Trinity, Christ and the sacraments, even though there may have been confusion of formulæ; yet she refused to bind herself by entering the Church.

Salvation and grace are normally linked to baptism and submission to the divine teaching. What are we to think about the case of Simone Weil? First we must recall a principle which is clear. It concerns what is generally known as good faith or sincerity, and has two aspects. The first states that any act which goes against the conscience is morally wrong. Saint Thomas confirms this by the most forcible example he can find: 'To believe in Christ is an excellent thing, and necessary to salvation, but the will can only adhere to it by the light of reason. If therefore the reason saw something wrong in it, the will would proceed towards it as towards something wrong, not that it is wrong in itself, but because the error of the reason would take it to be so.' We notice that supreme respect is given to the conscience and that this respect is of such a degree that, even when the conscience errs, we cannot act rightly by going against it.

The second aspect throws a new light on the subject. If good faith in error is to have such value, and if sincerity is to be of such price, it must be true sincerity. That person is not sincere who affirms or denies without reason, following his caprice or his passions; that person who has not taken the trouble to seek the truth or to pass beyond the point of view of his own interests or perhaps his attachments. Is a person sincere when he is the toy of his *ego* or when he makes no effort to be objective and well informed in matters affecting his conscience? . . .

Many kinds of so-called good faith are nothing but hypocrisy, or falsehood which is hiding from the light. Those in such a state add the sin of ignorance to their other faults. Sincerity presupposes a transparency to the light and an effort in the direction of truth which are not particularly easy.

But there are famous examples: Saint Paul, persecuting the Christians 'through ignorance', and 'zeal for God'; Newman, the future cardinal, holding on to the idea for years before his conversion that the Pope was Antichrist, and so on.

Bearing this in mind, there is no difficulty in supposing it to be possible, temporarily especially, for a person to accept false ideas which he thinks have been revealed, or to make a mistake and believe he is following the right road and so on. All this is what theology designates as invincible ignorance. Ignorance which cannot prevail against the truth of God, but for which the conscience cannot be blamed, on account of its good faith.

To come back to the case of Simone Weil; there can be no question of judging a conscience. In any special concrete case such judgments are always rash: what do we know of a conscience and of the extent to which the light proposed to it has penetrated? Personal experiences and impressions, philosophic culture, the influence of environment, physical temperament and psychological formation are so many factors which make it scarcely possible to catch any particular wavelengths without interference from others. Which of us ever really listens to the other speaker in a dialogue? How much of it remains in our memory? Simone seems to have felt this difficulty. 'Sometimes I cannot help repeating, fearfully and with regret, what he said to me. How am I to know whether I am remembering it exactly? He is not there to tell me' (Prologue).

Thus the rôle of a messenger is to repeat the words entrusted to him, carefully effacing himself so that he does not get in the way between the conscience to whom he is sent and the divine message; he will always tremble lest he be found unfaithful. . . .

As for the principle, it is perfectly clear: it is possible to be in good faith while opposing the Church.

What are we to deduct from this possibility of good faith and consequently of a state of grace and salvation for non-Christians? First, that we must not judge, and that our zeal for the truth must never become hostility for persons. Saint Augustine said very beautifully that we should combine 'the hatred of error and the love of those who err'. In the heart of a Christain there should be respect for his separated brother.

'But', it may be objected, 'does not such a conception diminish our apostolic zeal?' The question is, first of all, to decide whether the conception is true or not. Then we have to understand it thoroughly, and whoever understands it thoroughly will have all the more true zeal, zeal without bitterness but full of ardour; and the intensity of his ardour will be the greater the dearer the unbeliever is to God. The greater my respect, and even friendship for a being, the more I desire his truest good. Never would it enter my head to influence him with an unsound argument or to exert pressure on him through the weight or prestige of our friendship (that would be a lack of respect), but, at the same time, I long all the more intensely to bring him face to face with that truth which liberates and completes.

Subhuman methods of pressure and propaganda are out of the question and are all the more inconceivable the more living one's idea of the action of grace, for this action is infinitely holy and mysterious.

To meditate upon the spiritual journey, incomplete as it was, of Simone Weil can afford much food for reflection to those Catholics at least who want to attain to true wisdom in their service of God's kingdom.

It is also good for them to understand that Christ is a prodigal sower who throws his seed with generous universality. To doubt his action, either because the visible results do not correspond with our views or because human liberty obstructs it, is, it seems to me, to misunderstand his merciful wisdom. Why should we not admit that his grace, which awoke within Simone Weil that religious sentiment which was absolutely new to her, had by this very fact inspired her with respect and love for incomplete religious traditions? Why should we not admit also that the sense of holiness with which the experience of others begins was in her a result of the Meeting which changed her life, bringing an awareness of God's reality and the certitude of Christ? Why should we not admit that, for reasons unknown to us, this grace, which is so infinitely respectful of our liberty, our delays and our resistances, here seemed to leave its work uncompleted.

I agree that this is an extreme and difficult case, but it is not impossible. May those who are incapable of letting their attention rest on the mystery of the Church – the only means of salvation and the mysterious home of all souls living in God's friendship, even outside the visible fold – may those people be content to pray humbly for their brothers without judging them and without showing a narrow and sectarian spirit. This is neither the first nor the only time it has been possible for a Christian to recognize grace outside its usual setting . . . God is free in his gifts and his invitations.

From the above considerations it is evident that the illusion of a mistaken conscience is possible in conjunction with the grace of God. This is all the more possible to admit in the case of Simone Weil, since she never to my knowledge felt that she had reached her goal, and since she suffered deeply on account of her incompleteness. . . .

We might compare her essay on 'The Forms of the Implicit Love of God' with those words of Péguy concerning the anti-clericalism of his youth: 'Our invincible preallegiance, our youthful preallegiance, to the Christian way of life, to Christian poverty, to the deepest truths of the Gospel, our obstinate spontaneous and buoyant secret preallegiance, already constituted an invisible parish for us.

The difficulty which is probably insoluble is to distinguish the action of the Holy Spirit and the value of Simone's mystical experience: poetic genius, the power of concentration, psychological aptitude and the discipline of philosophical training can lead a soul high in the direction of what is known as 'premystical' to distinguish it from mysticism proper, that is to say the direct action of God manifesting God.

Thus the problem about Simone Weil once more arises: should we speak of that grace which in mercy invades the soul from outside or that which grows mysteriously from within?

This being said, and said in all seriousness, I do not see how we can doubt of the supernatural character of the illumination which changed the whole orientation of her thought, or how we can honestly refuse her testimony concerning God and his Christ.

For herself it was a certainty which never wavered or grew dim. It was her proof: 'In my arguments about the insolubility of the problem of God I had never foreseen the possibility of that, of a real contact, person to person, here below, between a human being and God' (Letter IV). She thought that it was a proof for others, 'the ontological proof', the 'proof by perfection' as she used to say and as she repeated in London. Everything combines to give this experience the force of irrecusable evidence: its unexpectedness, its opposition to the current of her thoughts and its lack of any connection with her psychological or metaphysical outlook, also its novelty, so utterly unlike any other experience: 'For already here below we receive the capacity for loving God and for representing him to ourselves with complete certainty as having the substance of real, eternal, perfect and infinite joy. Through our fleshly veils we receive from above presages of eternity which are enough to efface all doubts on this subject' (Letter VI).

But does she make of this a reason for going against the words of Our Lord, refusing baptism, depriving herself of his Bread and rejecting his Church? I do not think anyone could legitimately claim this if they referred back to her writings. She never ceased to stress the unique and contradictory character of what she considered to be her personal vocation. She thought she was intended to draw people to the Church; for instance, she congratulated a convert, saying: 'I see that really we are very near to each other.' She envied those who were in the Church.

Finally, and perhaps above all, she never ceased to repeat that she suffered from a sense of incompleteness, and to bring out the sacred character of her problem and, from the very fact that she was outside Christianity, she placed this problem before all men without having the means of solving it. Her message indicates the answer.

'To love with all one's mind is to guess where the hunger and thirst of the spirit lie and to provide for them' (E. Hello).

Note

1   All found in *Waiting on God* except the 'Prologue', which is in *Connaissance Surnaturelle*.

X.

HER MESSAGE

'I am separated from truth.' Simone Weil allowed herself to say this in order to explain her desire for death and her hope that in it she would find the truth she craved. Could any words be more poignant or more heart-rending?

In a sense it is true of every human being. The great Newman asked that the words 'Ex umbris et imaginibus in veritam'[1] should be inscribed on his tomb, and Saint Paul wrote: 'We see now through a glass in a dark manner: but then face to face. Now I know in part: but then I shall know even as I am known' (1 Cor. xiii. 12).

With Simone Weil there was, in addition, her sense of incompleteness, and the suffering of a mind torn in opposite directions; at the same time within the Church and outside it, anxious to obey and afraid of illusion; struggling in an impasse due to her adherence to the Catholic faith, her inability to conceive of it as an object of affirmation for her intellect, her inclination to jump to universal systematizations before testing the objective value of her material, and her scrupulous sincerity which drove her to give expression to every idea which came into her head before she had been able to check its value. Is it possible to speak of a message in the case of a mind which was still trying to find its way? Moreover this mind is scarcely known to us apart from rough notes which were never revised and upon which we have no light from any outside sources, confidences of friends or circumstantial details. Under these conditions is there not a danger of misrepresenting her thought and of attributing to her ideas which were never hers? Do we not risk giving the authority of her mind and spirit to what was perhaps nothing but the changing foam thrown off from reading or conversations (for she gives none too many references), objections to be refuted or material to be transformed in the process of assimilation?

It is necessary to do some careful sorting out in order to know her thoughts and also the truth of her thoughts. She herself invites us to do so. Those who would give her the authority of a master, either by accepting everything which comes from her as completely true, or, on the other hand, by contesting it all as a false doctrine, forget that she herself was only a traveller, journeying towards the truth.

Let us listen to her own warnings on this subject: 'Ideas come and settle in my mind by mistake, then, realizing their mistake, they absolutely insist on coming out. I do not know where they come from, nor what they are worth, but I do not think that I have the right to prevent this operation' (Letter IV, *Waiting on God*, page 32). 'It is obvious that I have no right to have a theory about the sacraments. But for this very reason, if such a theory enters my mind I am under an obligation to make it come out. It is for others to decide what it is worth and where it comes from' (unpublished London notes).

'I do not know what they are worth' . . . 'it is for others to decide what it is worth. . . . ' Yet, at the same time, a scruple in the strongest sense of the word, a psychological determination, in fact, forces her to give expression to everything: 'It is this obligation which forces me to write things which I know I have not personally the right to write' (ibid). And in another place she says, 'As, however, it is a fact that I have thought them [certain things which might offend], I dare not keep them from you' (Letter VI, *Waiting on God*, page 41).

To fail to do this sorting out would therefore be to imprison and stifle oneself with all the conflicts of which we have spoken. Personally, I think that the swirl of conflicting thoughts which has arisen around Simone Weil has somewhat distracted people's attention from what is positive in her. It is easy enough to underline her incoherences, her exaggerations and her contradictions. I have indeed dwelt here on her conflicts. These formed the substances of our dialogue, which was not a discussion so much as a striving after the truth (the texts of *Waiting on God* only represent a part of this striving and cannot be understood apart from it), but I have dwelt on these conflicts because I want to help to bring out what is positive in her and what is valid, in so far as this word can be applied to human thought.

It would, however, be rash to claim to make a complete inventory of the spiritual discoveries of Simone Weil, or even of those most definitely connected with Christianity; in her everything is connected with Christianity and the word discovery is hardly suitable, for the truths in question have been heard 'from the beginning', but she has said them again with a genius which is all her own and lived them with all the depth and force of her personality.

Perhaps at the head of the list we should put her doctrine of attention, whether applied to facts, ideas or persons ('Thoughts on the Right Use of School Studies with a View of the Love of God). Once the importance has been stressed of preliminary enquiry, knowledge stored in the memory, the attentive study of documents and examination of all the facts necessary to avoid rash, unreal or erroneous systematizations, once all these prerequisites have been stressed (although this was neither the object of the essay nor the main concern of the author), this attitude of opening to the truth makes the soul utterly transparent to the light, prepares the way for the most beautiful vocations and enable human eyes to become as the eyes of Christ. While most thinkers want to invent their truth, attention disposes us to receive it.

In spite of the difficulties which attended such a method for Simone Weil on account of her intellectual temperament, if I may put it in this way, I am convinced that she would have been able to reduce and, as it were, burn up from within most of the prejudices – chiefly of an historical nature – which hindered her search.

It is useless to insist upon it; many consider this paper to be Simone Weil's masterpiece: 'Attention consists of suspending our thought, leaving it detached, empty and ready to be penetrated by the object, it means holding in our minds, within reach of this thought, but on a lower level and not in contact with it, the diverse knowledge we have acquired which we are forced to make use of. Our thought should be, in relation to all particular and already formulated thoughts, as a man on a mountain who, as he looks forward, sees also below him, without actually looking at them, a great many forests and plains. Above all our thought should be empty, waiting, not seeking anything, but ready to receive in its naked truth the object which is to penetrate it' (*Waiting on God*, 'Thoughts on the Right Use of School Studies', page 56). 'We do not obtain the most precious gifts by going in search of them but by waiting for them. Man cannot discover them by his own powers, and if he sets out to seek for them he will find in their place counterfeits of which he will be unable to discern the falsity' (ibid., pages 56–7). 'This way of looking is, in the first place, attentive. The soul empties itself of all its own contents in order to receive the being it is looking at, just as he is, in all his truth. Only he who is capable of attention can do this' (ibid., page 59).

Another of the most beautiful features of Simone's doctrine is the attentive understanding of the individual in affliction: misfortune has made him like a thing, he is the nameless casualty, lying inert and bleeding by the wayside. We should respond to such affliction with compassion full of respect and attention, of devotion and insight, of self-loss through love of the sufferer, with compassion which is God's compassion in our human hearts.

That was one of her most cherished thoughts and one of the most generous motives of her life. Even those who feel obliged to censure her intellectual faults and her resistance to the words of Christ cannot help admiring the reckless devotion and heroism of her charity.

'That which you have done to the least of these my little ones. . . .'

We can dispute this or that of her formulæ: but she had been able to see for herself that only too often acting 'for God' went side by side with a complete lack of attention to the afflicted and the outcast: hence her concern. Moreover, when we read her closely we see what she meant, and understand that, from her point of view, to love the man in affliction and relieve him as we should, in a spirit of service and without a shadow of condescension, is not possible except supernaturally under the inspiration and though the very action of Christ.

It is obvious that the present time is ripe for such a message; the advance of laws and technics which aim at planning for everybody and relieving all poverty makes each being into a number, an anonymous individual, classified by government officials. Is it possible to see what will happen if this technical progress is not accompanied by 'an extra ration of soul', if the 'Great Beast' is not carried off by a huge pair of wings?

This love of Simone's for human beings tended, alas, to screen the divine light, but it finds, or rather it is waiting for, its place in the Christian synthesis, for the true Christian loves men and respects the human values brought to light by the Saviour 'who took his delight among the children of men'.

It was this attitude which made it possible for her to converse, and to converse on deep matters, with people who were totally different from herself. Have we sufficiently noticed how she formed friendships with simple folk despite their lack of culture? With X or Y, in spite of their political differences? In a world where men shut themselves up in their circles and their parties, pass their time in labelling others without reference to what they really have in them but for the mere pleasure of classifying, judging, condemning, separating and opposing, is it not worth remembering this characteristic of Simone's?

Her conception of the duty of sanctity and of the ideal of evangelical purity should also be studied and placed among her most beautiful thoughts.

Apparently forgetting what she had said elsewhere, and recognizing the moral superiority of Christianity (she puts conscience above ideas, especially when she is systematizing), she says: 'It seems to me that in reality, if I dare to say so, saintliness is the minimum for a Christian. It is for the Christian what honesty in money matters is for the merchant, bravery for the soldier, a critical mind for the scholar. The specific value of the Christian is saintliness – if not, what is it?'

She formed a very high idea of this saintliness; she frequently repeated that all illusion must be excluded, whatever its name. 'We must be careful about the level on which we place the infinite. If we place it on the level which is only suitable for the finite, it will matter very little what name we give it' (*Gravity and Grace*, pages 48–9).

But she also described its positive aspect: 'Truth which becomes life, that is the testimony of the spirit, truth transformed into life'

(*Connaissance Surnaturelle*, page 134). 'Sanctity is accompanied by an uninterrupted welling up of supernatural energy which acts irresistibly upon its surroundings. The other state (deceptive semblance) is accompanied with moral exhaustion, and often – as in my own case – exhaustion which is both physical and moral' (Letter to M. Schumann). She did not forget that fidelity is a gift of God and that all confidence in ourselves is a denial. Concerning Saint Peter's presumption she said: 'This was to deny Christ already for it was to suppose the source of fidelity to be in himself and not in grace' (*Connaissance Surnaturelle*, page 114). She tried elsewhere to explain the part played by effort and the gift of grace: 'For a man to be really inhabited by Christ as the host is after consecration, it is necessary that his flesh and blood should previously have become inert matter, and, what is more, food which his fellows can consume. Then, by a secret consecration, this matter can become the flesh and blood of Christ. This second transmutation is the affair of God alone, but the first is partly our own affair' (*Connaissance Surnaturelle*, page 41).

This brings us to her sense of God. It is perhaps the centre of her message. No doubt there are conceptions which might be disputed, exaggerated formulæ, such as the one against hope, deviations and resistances, since she rejects some of the divine commandments and seems sometimes to make the divinity impersonal, but for her God is truly God: 'The object of our desire must be none other than the one and only good, pure, perfect, total, absolute, inconceivable for us.' Many label with the word God a conception invented by their own soul or provided by their environment. Simone thirsted to contemplate God himself, to be 'in contact' with him, to depend upon him, to be transformed into him, whereas only too often religion becomes bogged in human elements and puerile conceptions.

Moreover, she knew that we can only go to God through the Mediator, and throughout the *Intuitions Pré-Chrétiennes* she insists upon this necessity: 'If we had chlorophyll we should feed on light as trees do. Christ is this light' (Connaissance Surnaturelle, page 245). She readily looked upon him as the model to be reproduced, or rather, as the life that animates us and the centre from which all the truth and light of the world proceed. At times some of her formulæ seem to be slipping into syncretism, but it must not be forgotten that she eagerly affirms the historical reality of the Incarnation and of the life of Our Lord and that if she searches for traces of him in all places it is because she wants to bring all things to him.

Note

[1] 'Out of the shadows and fancies into the truth.'

XI.

THE GREAT REQUEST

Considering only her incompleteness, her difficulties, which seem to them but slight, and the often unjustifiable accusations she made, forgetting the efforts of the former anarchist and volunteer on the Spanish front, most of Simone Weil's readers have passed over in silence the great request with which she ended her farewell letter: 'To-day it is not nearly enough merely to be a saint, but we must have the saintliness demanded by the present moment, a new saintliness, itself without precedent' ... 'Such a petition [for this saintliness] is legitimate, today at any rate, because it is necessary. I think that under this or any equivalent form it is the first thing we have to ask for now, we have to ask for it daily, hourly, like a famished child constantly asks for bread. The world needs saints who have genius, just as a plague-stricken town needs doctors. Where there is a need there is also an obligation' (Letter VI, *Waiting on God*, pages 45–6).

We had already spoken of this together; I had quoted Maritain's words, to which she alluded without understanding all they implied: 'a new style of saintliness, the sanctification of the secular'; but from far away in Casablanca, before a final silence brought our dialogue to a close, it was the appeal she sent out, it is the appeal she seems to be sending still.

She who knew the bitterness of the worker's lot, the miseries of revolution, the distresses in factories, universities and schools, in artistic circles and political circles, she who seems to have embodied and experienced within herself all the contemporary world as well as the whole of antiquity, she it is who makes this appeal to all who love God.

Simone was not thinking of genius in the ordinary sense of the word; she knew very well, and she said so, that the truest intelligence is to be found at the artisan's bench just as much as in the library of the intellectual, and that we can draw near to truth not only by study but by every form of human work. Genius meant to her the opening of the intelligence of man to the wisdom of God. Everyone is capable of that and that is what she asks:

Saintliness of genius, which applies all its intelligence to understand the message Christ entrusted to his Church for the entire world and which allows itself to be penetrated to its very depths by his searching and magnificent light.

Saintliness of genius, which seeks to understand the crying needs of an uprooted, impoverished world . . . and longs to discover a new incarnation in a spirituality of work, culture and study. . . .

Saintliness of genius, which strives to make use of its knowledge of the humanity of past ages, to trace hidden values, reflections of Christ and the expectation or the invisible presence of God.

Saintliness of genius, which seeks in contemporary humanity the testimony of a soul Christian by nature, waiting for Christ, and which discovers in all its values waiting stones, treasures to be integrated, outlines to be filled in or ways of expressing the worship that is 'in spirit and in truth'.

Saintliness of genius, which makes men live the life of the Church and present it both as personal, because it is the Home of our personal and immediate relationship with God, and universal, because it has a visible or invisible relation to all men; for it is the Presence of the Spirit and the new Humanity.

Saintliness of genius, such as the world cries out for in these times without precedent – saintliness which cannot be only for one but should be for all Christians, saintliness for scholars, particularly those who make a study of the history of religions, and also for politicians who are called upon to build the new world; saintliness for colonists, who should have a sense of man's nature and of their responsibility with regard to civilizations which have to be preserved and developed; saintliness for missionaries above all, missionaries to give the Body of Christ its true dimensions and, already here on earth, to make it all in all.

Saintliness of genius, which craves for understanding and intelligence in order to show to all men that Christ is the Truth.

Saintliness to which nothing human or divine is foreign or unfamiliar, so that each one feels at home with it and thus enters the home of God.

Saintliness of genius enabling us to understand others and to shoulder their load, instead of leaving them lying by the roadside.

Saintliness of genius for each one of us, so that in this being beside us who has 'the colour of a dead leaf and does not exist', we may recognize a sincerity which is struggling and which Christ calls; so that having in us the 'fullness of God', we may understand and help her incompleteness, respect her efforts, clumsy though they may be, and love her with all the love we have received.

Part Two
by Gustave Thibon

HOW SIMONE WEIL
APPEARED TO ME

This title has a very precise meaning for me. I am going to try to speak of Simone Weil herself, disregarding the immense halo of commentaries, discussions and legends which surround her. For a moment I am going to forget even her writings in order to call back to life that unknown being who, as it were, dropped from the sky and for a brief space shared my existence. We are too apt to forget that the illustrious dead were living people like ourselves – '*en situation*' (in concrete surroundings) as Gabriel Marcel would say – involved in the order of time and space and subject to admixture and limitations. Fame reduces them to the state of timeless abstractions; it hangs on the wall of history a few pictures around which gravitate more or less arbitrary reconstructions, interpretations and disputes – endless discussions and battles of ideas, which have little more connection with the real being who gave rise to them than an avalanche has with the breath of wind and the loose stones which set it in motion. Biographies themselves suffer from glory's conformism; the ideas which a dead man heralded come between the narrator and his facts. Instead of receiving these facts in their original spontaneity and their often irreducible diversity, he tends to insert them into ready-made frameworks and to force them into the artificial unity demanded by the legend. Thus the *simplicity* of the testimony disappears – in favour of the *over-simplified* interpretation. I should like to break these abstract frameworks and these distorting glasses for a while in order to present an unadorned likeness of Simone Weil – the likeness of a living person in contact with other living persons. I want to keep clear of all apriorism or prejudice – including the prejudice of friendship – for friendship itself comes after knowledge: *de ignotis nulla cupido*. . . .

This portrait may appear complex and contradictory. I cannot help that. Life itself is a tissue of contrasts, and the greatest men are those who embrace in the unity of their nature the most diverse and opposite elements. Vauvenargues' words are very much to the point here: 'We are quite wrong to consider the union of good and evil as monstrous or enigmatic; it is for lack of penetration that we can reconcile so few things'. The slightest experience of life teaches us that none but imbeciles or the heroes of bad novels are 'all of a piece'. Simone Weil was not an imbecile and, putting aside all false modesty, I do not think I am enough of one myself to reduce her to what is but a single aspect of her character or a single dimension of her genius. Moreover, the very nature of our friendship, which of itself made anything cheap or ungenerous between us impossible, was equally opposed to unconditional praise or the artificial flowers of panegyric. This friendship, indeed, never lessened the distance which separated our minds or the respective independence of our judgments. 'It is essential', she once wrote to me, 'that divergences should not lessen friendship and that friendship should not grow by lessening divergences.' There could be no better expression of the nuptial pact between love and justice. . . .

I will, then, evoke the Simone Weil whom I welcomed under my roof, with whom I cultivated the soil and broke bread just ten years ago – before she became the very thing of which she had most horror: a famous personage. To those who, dazzled by her reputation, find too many shadows in my portrait, I would reply that pure light only exists in God, the 'sun of spirits', and that it is not good to let ourselves become dazzled by the projectors of fame. Simone Weil used often to say that most of those who bow before the glory of Joan of Arc would have condemned her as a heretic and a witch during her life. The same is true on a different scale of Simone Weil herself. With the exception of a few rare admirers and friends of the first days, I must own that those who knew her in 1941 generally spoke to me of her as an anarchist, a visionary, and an impossible person – and I am deliberately softening the expressions they used. And now, these are the very people who flatter themselves that they discerned her genius and her heroism from the very first!

Their judgment, enslaved by the power of public opinion, has simply varied with the reactions of the 'Great Beast', which, like the 'crowd' of Victor Hugo, 'has too many eyes to be able to look, too many heads to have a thought'. Let us try to be more balanced. . . .

I will lay bare my evidence. This does not mean that it will be perfect, its great drawback will be precisely that it is *my* evidence. I can speak only of what I have seen, but from the very fact that it was *I* who saw it, my limitations and my preferences will colour my impressions. Besides this, talking about oneself is always a hard trial both for the modesty of the speaker and the patience of the listener – and how can one help doing so when recalling a meeting or a conversation? It is, indeed, for this reason that all literature which is in any way connected with memoirs is at the same time so attractive and so disappointing: it is attractive because it is the testimony of a witness, and it is disappointing because the personality of the witness usually takes up too much room. In such cases, everything depends on the direction of the lighting. I once heard a witty woman complaining about the description a pedant had just given us of his travels in Andalusia. His hearers were literally bowed down by the weight of all the 'I saw', 'I said', 'I did' . . . and when I argued, though without conviction, 'After all he can only speak of what he has seen', she replied: 'Of course, but he does not talk about Granada which he has seen, but of himself who has seen Granada.' That is what the question turns on. Every witness is obliged to say: 'I saw.' What matters is whether he places the accent on the *I* or the *saw*, on the subject or the object. May those angels who restrain our self-complacency and absurdity keep me from speaking about myself in writing of Simone Weil!

* * *

I have described in the preface of *La Pesanteur et la Grace* (*Gravity and Grace*), the circumstances which led to my meeting with Simone Weil. My old friend, the Reverend Father Perrin, had asked me to have her to stay in order to initiate her into life on the land. I find it very hard now to distinguish the motives which made me say yes. No doubt the first was a desire not to refuse my friend. It must also be admitted, since kindness in the pure state can scarcely be said to exist, that I was still at that time of life when one is eager to make new friends. In the few letters which Simone wrote to me at that period giving details of the requirements of her temporary vocation as a land girl, it was possible already to trace two great contradictory motives. It was the tension between these motives which caused her to have such heart-rending experience of human misery and the cross, and at the same time prevented her from attaining to supreme serenity. On the one hand there was a longing for absolute self-effacement, an unlimited opening to reality even under its harshest forms, and, on the other, a terrible self-will at the very heart of the self-stripping; the inflexible desire that this stripping should be her own work and should be accomplished in her own way, the consuming temptation to verify everything from within, to test everything and experience everything for herself.

In the first letter that I received from her she already showed the unshakable resolution to engage her whole being upon the route she had traced: 'I ardently wish to be able to do all that may be asked of me, without benefiting by any consideration. . . . I am not worrying as to the consequences of such work, but as to whether I shall be able to carry it out. I can only long to find the necessary force within me. . . . In any case I hope not to fail in that resolution which enables one to go to the very limit of one's strength. . . . '

The principle of the Nothing and the All which dominated the whole life of Simone Weil is found to be the basis of her agricultural vocation.

She wanted first to become empty of self by giving herself entirely to work – to find out from experience what soul and thought become in a being whose time and strength are ceaselessly used up by hard obligatory labour. . . . 'I want my time and the current of my thoughts, in so far as they depend on my body, to be subjected to the same necessities as those which weigh upon no matter what farm-hand – that is to say: weariness and the compulsory task. . . . I think that intellectual culture, far from giving a right to privileges, constitutes in itself a privilege which is almost frightening and which involves terrible responsibilities per contra. . . . I want to prove to myself that I think this way by shouldering, for a time at any rate, a burden such as those who have no share in this privilege have to bear all their lives.'

She hoped also – since emptiness attracts plenitude – that earth and nature, to which she wanted to give herself completely, would perhaps give themselves to her in return and, when she was at that extreme point of physical weariness which suspends the activities of the self, would allow her to taste their deep and ineffable reality: 'Perhaps, in addition, it may be given me, at least for a few moments, to receive the reward attached to work on the land and to none other, the feeling that the earth, the sun, the landscape really exist and are something more than mere scenery. This sense of reality, though it only lasts for a second, amply repays days and days of the bitterest fatigue and, to judge from my own experience, it is only granted when one has been working. But I do not allow myself to desire this, and scarcely even to think of it; for the earth only surrenders to those who have a claim . . . to those who have given their lives, and I do not want to indulge myself in literature after the style of Giono. . . . '

After a short exchange of letters Simone Weil arrived, for I had proposed that she should spend a few weeks with me in order to learn about the different kinds of agricultural work while she was waiting to become a real farm-hand under a large landowner of the district. How can I describe this first interview? I do not want to talk about her physical appearance – she was not ugly, as has been said, but prematurely bent and old-looking through asceticism and illness, and her magnificent eyes alone triumphed in this shipwreck of beauty. Nor will I dwell on the way she was turned out and her unbelievable luggage – she had a superb ignorance, not only as to the canons of elegance, but extending to the elementary practices which enable a person to pass unnoticed. I will merely say that this first contact aroused feelings in me which, though certainly quite different from antipathy, were none the less painful. I had the impression of being face to face with an individual who was radically foreign to all my ways of feeling and thinking and to all that, for me, represents the meaning and savour of life. It was, in short, the revelation of my own antipodes; I felt a stranger in a strange land, faced with a new world and unknown skies. I did not yet know that, though we were not following the same star, our souls would meet in the same heaven. My only positive impression was a sense of unreserved respect for someone whose unique stature I dimly discerned despite all our intellectual and emotional divergences. This feeling of veneration increased still more when, after having left her for a few moments to receive a visitor, I returned to find her sitting on a tree-trunk in front of the house, lost in contemplation of the valley of the Rhône. Then I saw her gaze gradually emerge from the vision in order to come back to ordinary sight; the intensity and the purity of that gaze were such that one felt that she was contemplating interior depths at the same time as the magnificent perspective which opened at her feet, and that the beauty of her soul corresponded with the tender majesty of the landscape.

A more rugged side of her character showed itself as soon as we had to proceed to the question of her new quarters. Finding our modest house too comfortable, she refused the room I was offering her and wanted at all costs to sleep out of doors. Then it was I who became vexed, and after long discussions she ended by giving way. The next day a compromise was reached. At that time my wife's parents had a little half-ruined house on the banks of the Rhône and we settled her in there, not without a few complications for everybody. It would all have been so much simpler otherwise! I could mention a hundred characteristics of the same kind: she, who when her pleasure or her needs were involved would not have allowed anyone to make the slightest sacrifice on her behalf, did not seem to realize the complications and even sufferings she caused in the lives of others as soon as there was a question of her vocation to self-effacement. Her own eagerness for discomfort in little things and affliction in great ones made her oblivious of the splashes of discomfort and affliction which might bespatter her surroundings. Perhaps, also, her humility made her think that as she was not worthy of being loved, there was little risk of others suffering on her account. One day, after having asked me to intervene with the Vichy authorities on behalf of a Spanish refugee who had been deported to Algiers, she suddenly asked me to swear to her that I would do nothing for her should she be imprisoned in her turn. I protested – only the evening before her parents had made me promise the exact contrary. Finally I said to her: 'Let us reverse the

rôles: would you be happy if I were in prison while you were free?'
She raised her head a little and replied with a suppressed light
in her eyes: 'I could not endure it.' I think these were the most
affectionate words she ever said to me. But, when faced with
the possibility of the same suffering – the passive witnessing of the
affliction of a beloved being – why did she measure with so unequal
a balance? There I had, as it were, an icy foretaste of the transcendental egoism of heroes. . . .

What I have just said is very severe – and it needs all the more
shading because it is true in part. 'The religious man thinks only of
himself,' said Nietzsche. That is true in every sense of those pious
folk of an inferior order who neglect their most obvious duties to
follow an imaginary vocation, and it is still true *in one sense* of
heroes and saints who have not achieved within themselves the
supreme self-surrender. I am well aware that it is not egoism to obey
God rather than men, and that those under great inspiration have
something better to do than to worry about the scratches and even
the wounds which their docility to the Spirit may cause among the
poor beings whom chance has placed near them. I know also that
this uncomfortable side of Simone Weil's character was not peculiar
to her but is common to many heroic souls – who was that kindly
bishop who wanted to add to the Litany of the Saints the invo-
cation: 'From living saints, Good Lord deliver us'? A Francis
of Assisi or a Joan of Arc in responding to their distant vocation
would never hesitate to make their immediate neighbour suffer. I
know all that and yet, none the less, I think that in the particular
case of Simone Weil the tension and the rigidity of her obedience
to her vocation were a sign, not indeed of unauthenticity, but of the
green immaturity of her spiritual life. The best fruit remains hard
as long as it is green. . . .

This notion of immaturity seems to me particularly valuable for
the elucidation of certain contrasts in the behaviour and thought
of Simone Weil – and in the first place the enigma of her double
attitude with regard to herself and with regard to her neighbour.
Her aim was self-forgetfulness, and she came upon herself in this
very forgetfulness; she loved her neighbour with all her being, and
in her devotion she too often overlooked the real desires and needs
of others.

Someone has described Rimbaud as 'a mystic in the wild state'. Such a judgment can only be applied in a very indirect manner to Simone Weil. I have, however, often wondered how far certain very subtle values of western civilization had penetrated to the deepest levels of her nature. What she lacked was that suppleness with regard to destiny, that healthy scepticism, that superior irony before the vicissitudes of the human comedy, that aristocratic standing back from oneself and others which is surprised at nothing, and, above all, that spontaneous and actual sense of proportion which makes it possible to see everything in its right relationship and to attain to a universal comprehension and benevolence. No doubt she owed this hardness of green fruit (maturity softens and detaches . . .) to her racial origin; she was indeed the daughter of that people marked with the sign of contradiction – that 'stiff-necked' people whom the prophets sought to unbend – and her passionate anti-semitism is the most striking evidence of her descent. Is there anything more Jewish than the perpetual tension and uneasiness, the urge to examine and test the great realities – and the feverish search for eternity in the time order wherein we can recognize in the noblest representatives of this chosen and rebellious race the ancient impatience for the Promised Land and a temporal kingdom? From this point of view the case of Simone Weil is somewhat like that of Spinoza. She was passionate in her 'very scorn for the passions; she was still searching for a sign in her refusal of all signs. This soul, who wanted to be flexible to every movement of the divine will, could not bear the course of events or the kindness of her friends to change by one inch the position of the stakes with which her own will had marked her path of immolation. Though utterly and entirely detached from her tastes and needs, she was not detached from her detachment. And the way she mounted guard around her emptiness still showed a terrible preoccupation with herself. In the great book of the universe spread often before her, her *ego* was, as it were, a word which she may perhaps have succeeded in *effacing*, but which was still *underlined*.

This failure to open to external reality, this determination to reconstruct the world in accordance with the facts of her own experience, this categorical refusal of every truth which she had not elaborated and tested within her own mind – all these symptoms of immaturity have caused her to be accused of pride. I prefer not to give an opinion on this point; pride, which is the most inward of sins, can only be seen by God. What I can say is that I never saw any outward signs of it in her case. The most blunt contradictions or the refusal no less blunt to continue a discussion – two things of which I made a habit with her – did not meet with those expressions of wounded self-love which in the intellectual world are still more frequent than expressions of intelligence itself. I always found her unshakable (she was, as it were, barred and bolted in her opinions), I never found her touchy. I repeat that she could be as hard and unyielding as green fruit; but she was not proud. . . .

The saints are not given us for the sake of comfort, and I do not entirely reproach her for this uncomfortable side of her nature. Moreover there were some delightful moments when she let herself go and relaxed. Yet she lacked that supreme peace of mind, that sweetness and all-embracing indulgence which are the signs of God's maturity in man: the sharpness of green fruit was also hers! In what other way can we explain the harsh judgments and aversions which at times amazed me to the point of scandal? She told me one day that she would refuse to shake hands with any man whom she knew to frequent the houses of prostitutes. Again, the day after her arrival at my house, as we were opening the daily papers which announced the death of one of Mussolini's sons in an aviation accident, she exclaimed: 'There you have one of the few men to whom I wish harm!' I have known at least one man who, at the end of his life, appeared to me to have attained total union with God: such words and such sentiments would have been impossible with him. What then did Simone Weil make of that supernatural love of which she expressed in a splendid sentence the necessary universality: 'To love men in the same way as the sun would love us if it saw us?' I found out later that her hatred was only an expression of the green immaturity and impatience of her love. . . .

The same isolation in her interior life tended to warp her relations with her neighbour. To be sure Simone Weil was one of those people for whom a neighbour does really exist; she was ready to make any sacrifices for him, but, though she had to a very high degree a sense of the other person *as someone preferable to herself*, she was very far from possessing to the same degree a sense of the other person *as someone else*. She was inwardly founded on love like those volcanoes of the arctic regions of which the lava is hidden under a covering of ice, but at the periphery she lacked that permeability and tenderness which enable us to know and love our brothers just as they are. A whole side of her conduct is explained by this tragic mingling of subjectivism and love which caused her to project her own *ego* into others so that she might then immolate herself to the phantom.

Her simplicity and capacity for illusion in psychological matters were unlimited. I have spoken elsewhere of her high-grade equalitarianism, that kind of 'levelling up' which led her to judge the souls and needs of others from what she experienced at her own altitude. From her project to make the teaching of Greek compulsory in elementary schools to the spiritual vocations she claimed to have discovered in people with the most colourless or vulgar outlook – how many wild fancies sprang from the transposition of her inner flame! How many times I heard her debating endlessly and to no purpose with Peter or Paul, presenting her bewildered hearer with arguments which had no meaning for anyone but herself? If there is a gospel sentence from which she failed to profit, it is most certainly that in which Christ tells us not to cast our pearls before swine. It is true that she had no fear of the answering clamour of angry grunts. . . .

One of the most striking forms which her respect for her neighbour took consisted of saying to all and sundry – with none too much regard for time or place – what she thought to be the truth. She refused to admit that truth is an elixir of which the doses have to be measured – lest it prove a poison. In this respect she went further than God himself, who wraps himself in so many veils and who told his disciples: 'I have still many things to say unto you, but you cannot bear them now.' It is only too easy to guess that this frankness, in season and out of season, wounded a great many vanities and roused strong antipathy for her in some quarters. Personally I have nothing to complain of in this respect, for, from the beginning, our friendship knew no eclipse and went on increasing until the time of our separation.

Our first contacts were rather hard. Our temperaments were very unlike and we were far from having the same tastes in art or the same opinions in philosophy and politics. . . . I can still hear her describing Victor Hugo as a sonorous imbecile and protesting loudly every time I expressed my admiration for Nietzsche. My esteem for the teaching of an eminent contemporary philosopher – whose name I will not mention as he long ago ceased to be my friend – roused her no less. One day she seized one of his books, read a few sentences aloud and ended up by saying with an air of defiance: 'You must admit that it is impossible to have a fine soul when one writes so badly!' All the passionate apriorism of Simone Weil is expressed in that exclamation. . . . In political matters it was scarcely any better. The atmosphere of discord and division which pervaded France at that time is well known. Without mixing directly in political action, I recognized the legitimacy of the Vichy Government, whereas Simone Weil was already a whole-hearted *'résistante'*. There was no element of agreement there, but I must admit that it never led to discord between us. Simone Weil, aware of the eminently relative character of political choice, which is concerned with seeking not perfection but the lesser evil, never showed the slightest intolerance towards me and did not hold my preferences against me. I have since learned that later on, in America, she defended the poor 'Vichyists' against the final and unqualified anathema fulminated by certain emigrants.

At about this time she went away for a few days in order to accompany her parents to the Alps. Before going, she asked me to let her have all my unpublished work so that she could read it quietly. Shortly afterwards I received a very long letter of which I will reproduce only the most significant passages here:

'I shall soon be coming back, but I am glad that this short absence gives me an opportunity to send you a letter, so that I can write things which a certain embarrassment and an invincible reserve prevent me from saying to you. . . . The first is that I cannot find adequate words to thank you for your kindness to me – with just this one reserve, that it far exceeds all reasonable measure. . . . This month has done me a great deal of good, physically and morally. . . . The second thing I want to say has to do with your

115

writings. . . . They contain, to my mind, some things of the highest order (which for me means a great deal); but not very many; not nearly as many as the praise of your friends suggests. You fully realize, for you know me well enough for that, that in such judgments no consideration can prevent me from being as honest as it is in my power to be. This does not only mean that I am sincere, which goes without saying, but that friendship, gratitude and sentiments of such a kind cannot serve to diminish but only to augment my scrupulous care and attention in trying to make a right evaluation. . . . You have already experienced the dark night, but it is my belief that a great deal of it still remains for you to pass through before giving your true measure; for you are far from having attained in expression, and hence in thought, to the degree of utter stripping, nakedness and piercing force which is indispensable to the style which belongs to you. From this point of view your last texts are much better and even contain some phrases which are more or less satisfying. Yet, on the whole, my feeling is still the same. . . . To tell you that you still have to pass through some of the dark night is to imply that you have in you, as a thinker and a writer, something more, something which goes beyond and above what appears on the paper, for otherwise there would not be any dark night to endure. I suppose this to be the case and that is why I am writing to you as I do, but I cannot know for certain. If I am right in supposing it, I am also right in writing to you in this way, and it may even be that more harshness would be better. . . . On the other hand, if I am mistaken, and if you have in you nothing more in the order of written thought which is asking to pass from within outwards through a thousand sufferings, I shall have been wrong in writing thus; and the fact of having friendship and gratitude as motives will in no way diminish my fault. Perhaps in that case you would not be able to help bearing me resentment for it, even without owning it to yourself. Therefore I am running a risk, for your friendship is precious to me – all the more so since, as I have no sense whatever of deserving it, it appears to me as a gratuitous gift. . . . '

Simone Weil owned to me afterwards that she had been almost certain that my friendship would not survive this douche of sincerity. Nothing of the sort. I was, on the contrary, infinitely grateful for her insight and her frankness (as a matter of fact true criticism is something as stimulating as true praise; but, alas! it is equally rare and we are generally praised or blamed for the wrong things). After this she conceived an exaggerated esteem for my 'modesty', when in reality something quite different was involved: if I am not very prone to literary vanity, it is perhaps because I have faults which are more real and exacting and which require more nourishment than a puff of smoke. Nietzsche has already spoken of the incredible modesty of the vain: it does indeed take little to satisfy them – a nothing or less than nothing, for the falsehood on which they feed is lower even than nothingness.

* * *

Thus the days passed by as we worked. Simone Weil came up each morning from her 'fairy-tale house' on the banks of the Rhône; I initiated her in the work of the fields, where her clumsiness was only equalled by her goodwill – the latter ended by triumphing over the former; we talked interminably; every evening she would sit on a stone bench near the fountain – in the very place where she first felt the reality of God as she repeated the 'Our Father' – and there she read Plato to me for long stretches, supporting the halting steps of the poor Greek scholar that I am with a thousand explanations. Her gifts as a teacher were tremendous: if she was inclined to over-estimate the possibilities of culture in all men, she knew how to place herself on the level of no matter what pupil in order to teach no matter what subject. I can imagine her carrying out the duties of an elementary school teacher just as well as those of a university professor! Whether she was teaching the rule of three to a backward village urchin or initiating me to the arcana of Platonic philosophy, she brought to the task and tried to obtain from her pupil that quality of extreme attention which, in her doctrine, is closely associated with prayer.

Sometimes she shared our meals, but she usually refused those things which town-dwellers could not have: to make her accept an egg was no easy task. Some days she did not appear at table and fed on the wild fruit she found in the countryside. She kept strictly to the ration regulations and would not admit that, even to help a neighbour, one should obtain the least commodity by unlawful means. One day when I was saying to her that I could not understand this loyalty to a government of which she did not recognize the legitimacy, she replied: 'We owe obedience to the powers that be in all things which do not compromise our conscience; if I were to carry out the ideological and political recommendations of Vichy, I should soil my soul, but in observing its rules concerning rationing, I only risk, at the very most, dying of hunger, and that is not a sin.' I remember having the utmost difficulty in calming her indignation against a baker of the district who generously offered her a little bread without coupons. Another day she declared that she was going to write to Admiral Leahy to suggest that he should intervene in order to stop the deliveries of corn to France: she based her request on the fact that most French people were Gaullists and that it was immoral that they should enjoy material advantages granted by a government which in their heart they condemned. . . .

All this – besides a certain aura of strangeness and melancholy which emanated from her and contributed even more to her personality than her words and actions – was not exactly restful. It was only very rarely that I had a sense of absolute relaxation in her presence. I am quite aware that the mere fact of knowing and loving someone who is superior to oneself necessarily creates a tension: nothing is more likely to produce storms than differences of altitude and of atmospheric pressure! But there are two kinds of higher souls. There are those who remain at their own level and isolate themselves there, and those who, raised to the heavens through love, know how to return to earth through pity. Simone Weil belonged to the second category through her ideal (no one has spoken better than she did of the descending movement of Grace which espouses and redeems Gravity) but by nature she tended towards the former. The tautness of a superhuman effort, the keen air and the vertigo of high summits emanated from her and always created a certain uneasiness in those around her. Her very elevation of soul appeared as a kind of unconscious defiance of mediocrity; before her, one felt stripped bare, pierced through and through and wholly delivered to the 'light with pitiless weapons' of the poet. This explains how her saintliness and radiance could at times wound. She had not yet reached the *reversed summit* of supreme humility, that point where height and depth correspond, that divine abasement which counterbalances man's baseness, that final simplicity in which the saint no longer judges anything but bathes all in the unity of love, and which makes it possible for the lowliest to approach the greatest without effort and without humiliation. Simone Weil was complete truth and, at a certain level, complete love; she was not yet complete welcome. Purity is in itself wounding; the mere presence of a saint makes the scars of old sins begin to bleed again – and only an infinite gentleness and compassion can dress those wounds which light causes.

In a sense she remained all her life the inflexible child who sat down in the snow and refused to go on because her parents had given the heaviest baggage to her brother to carry. This tension, this stubborn harshness, is apparent even in her style, and when I pointed this out to her one day she replied: 'Your criticism is certainly right. Awkwardness and stiffness are unquestionably faults; but I must own that of all faults they displease me the least, because it seems to me that one finds awkwardness and stiffness in the beautiful things that are most dear to me: Romanesque sculpture, the frescoes of Giotto, Greek sculpture of the early fifth century, Homer, Gregorian plain-song, in all those things, in short, which come a little before the point of classical maturity. It is not that I want to be compared with them.' Grace alone could have succeeded in giving flexibility to the hard edges of this character and of this diamond-like intelligence.

Fortunately this hardness had eclipses. To be sure Simone Weil never possessed that suppleness of character and that gift of spontaneity and familiarity which inspire sympathy and immediately put people at their ease. Her awkward stiffness showed even in her physical bearing: her attitudes, her gestures and the tone of her voice were full of it. The way she held the plates when washing up, which was as careful as it was unnatural, was enough to set me off in fits of irresistible laughter. Moreover she knew nothing of the demonstrative bodily side of affection and tenderness: kisses and embraces disgusted her and I never saw her cry. But she had exquisite moments of relaxation before a beautiful landscape or a work of art; she knew how to share in a family festivity, would joke with her friends and even occasionally allow herself some slight bodily treat. The Achilles' heel of her asceticism was smoking. Of all the things belonging to material life, tobacco was the only one which she was almost certain to accept. I can still see the expression on her face when I asked her one day 'to have the kindness' to go and fetch the tobacco from the next room. 'There is no need for kindness; the lowest concupiscence is enough.' And this is how she replied to a little parcel of cigarettes: 'Thank you very, very much. . . . This smoke has been transformed into pages covered with writing in my exercise books; but what is their value? That is another question. In any case their value cannot be great enough to justify your denying yourself for me.' Another time, just before her return to Marseilles, as she was counting out before me the money she had heroically earned during the grape harvest, I told her that I had no illusions about the destination of this sum, whereupon she replied with disarming spontaneity: 'But I shall certainly *also* buy a few books!' Of all the pictures I have kept in my mind of Simone Weil, no other moves me so much as that one. It is in those moments when the hero, the saint, or the God embraces the needs and weaknesses of men that his greatness is brought home to us most clearly and penetratingly. When Christ says, 'I thirst', these humble words remind us of the tenderly fraternal aspect of the inaccessible being who proclaimed, 'I am the Beginning.' *Quaerens me sedisti lassus*: God is never so fully God for us as when, clothed in flesh and the prisoner of time, he bows under the weight of the necessity he has created:

> *Ce Dieu qui décréta la mesure et le nombre*
> *Et mit sur l'Univers l'ordre que rien n'émeut,*
> *Le voici sous le poids de sa création. . . .*
> *De la chair et des jours, il a porté l'outrage,*
> *Il connait les tourments de l'amour exilé*
> *Qui se débat, tremblant, dans les serres de l'heure,*
> *L'Unique et l'éphémère en lui sout confondus. . . .* [1]

There is the whole mystery of the Incarnation: the impossible made flesh and the light transformed into food form the Ark of the Covenant between the human and the divine.

* * *

At the end of September 1941, Simone Weil, weary of the 'fairy-tale' life she led with us, joined a team of harvesters at Saint Julien de Peyrolas. To tell the truth she was not treated as an anonymous labourer; her employers put her up in their house and she had her meals with them; she even had long 'philosophical' conversations with them, of which we find echoes in her notebooks, about agricultural work and the meaning of property. But at work she was not given any special consideration and shared the lot of the labourers in everything. She had been afraid that she would not be able to accomplish the whole of this work which she started upon in bad physical condition. Actually she was able to hold out until the end of the harvest and even found it possible to study and write in the evenings. The constancy of her effort was inflexible: she was never behind her companions by the space of a single plant. Her only pair of shoes (canvas sandals) having worn out, some sabots were found for her. They fitted her badly and the strap made her ankles bleed and left a mark on them in two places. She did not lose an hour of labour on account of this suffering. Her employer, who witnessed her heroic determination without in any way understanding its true motives, told me about this, condensing his blind admiration into one phrase: 'She has pluck!'

When the grape harvest was over, she spent a few more days with us. Her parents, who were already preparing for their departure to America, called her back to Marseilles where her presence was necessary for obtaining some visa or other. The departure did not take place till six months later, after many alternating hopes and disappointments. This period of uncertainty and waiting was one of the most fruitful of her existence: the exercise books in which she noted down her thoughts contain the material for several volumes, she also gave lectures, carried on an enormous corre-spondence, etc. Moreover all this spiritual opening out coincided with an extreme anxiety about the future – a very special kind of anxiety which was peculiar to her: at a time when people like herself had every right to seek ways of avoiding the worst, her chief concern was how to draw down the worst upon her head. She valued risk as others do good fortune, she was afraid of being saved from harm in spite of herself. The mere thought that she should leave France to enslavement and woe and go to live safe from the threatening persecutions was enough to plunge her into despair. And if finally the balance was turned in favour of America, it was because she thought that her brief stay there would open up deeper possibilities of abasement and affliction (which was in fact what happened). But she hesitated for a long time and I even heard her compare herself to the ass of Buridan because she could not manage to decide between two pecks of affliction.

At those times when her departure seemed to her to be improbable, she made it her business to look out for agricultural work which would be harder and more anonymous than that of the previous summer. 'The Spring is coming,' she wrote to me. 'If I do not go, I want to work. May I ask you to start now to find me something? Do not pay any attention to the injunctions Father Perrin gave you last summer to find me something where the conditions of life are not too hard. He did not know me at that time; I think that now he would tell you that those injunctions no longer count. Find me anything: only let it be a place where they will be a long time before they find out that I am a doctor's daughter, an intellectual, etc. If I hit upon a place where the life is intolerable, there is nothing to prove that that will be bad for me. . . . I shall be extremely grateful to you if you will try to find me what is really an ordinary sort of place. . . . That presupposes a sort of heroism in friendship. I do not think that you are incapable of it. . . . '

I often reproached her with a lack of simplicity for thus sifting her destiny, instead of taking whatever came to her – the joys with the sorrows. I reproached her with putting as much study and calculation into the pursuit of affliction as mediocre souls do into their search for comfort and pleasure: after a certain altitude has been reached, the choice of man always limits the gifts of God. She replied that her vocation was to go to God through affliction and nothingness. What the respective parts of the human and the divine were in this attitude, is known only to God. People have found it possible to speak of a 'pathological predisposition to suffering' in connection with Simone Weil. That does not amount to very much: purely psychological explanations, when applied to anyone of such dimensions, suggest a garment that is absurdly tight and splits in all directions. It must also be observed that she did not set up her special vocation as a universal law. 'There are souls for whom everything here on earth which brings God nearer is salutary; for me it is everything which keeps him at a distance.' She could therefore conceive of other ways of going to God besides affliction; in particular, the vocation to perfect joy which dissolves the self in the same way as the purest suffering does. It is this joy which leaves 'in the soul filled by the object, no corner available for saying "I"'. She wrote to me in 1941: 'I do not approve of your sentence about happiness: "Do not be in a hurry to pity the man who is happy; perhaps he has not deserved anything better"; it is witty, but I do not think it is sound. I believe that true happiness is something no less rare and no less precious than pure and fruitful suffering. Some souls have the vocation of happiness; I do not envy them, but I admire them, and, when I think I have met one of them, I desire passionately that circumstances may favour him.' But what is the good of insisting on what is only an apparent opposition? Simone Weil knew unmixed joy in the same measure as she experienced pure suffering. Joy and suffering are not two antagonistic realities, but the two poles of one and the same reality which is called love. Circumstances cause us to pass from one to the other of these poles, but the substance of love does not vary.

Simone Weil constantly repeated these great truths to me to console me about her departure. She sailed for New York in May 1942. Shortly before our separation, I saw her again at Marseilles and we passed the greater part of the night together. To recall the details of this last conversation and to make of it just a memory among others seems to me a profanation today; things which pass beyond time cannot be confined to the memory. I will only say that I had the impression of being in the presence of an absolutely transparent soul which was ready to be reabsorbed into original light. I can still hear Simone Weil's voice in the deserted streets of Marseilles as she took me back to my hotel in the early hours of the morning; she was speaking of the Gospel; her mouth uttered thoughts as a tree gives its fruit, her words did not express reality, they poured it into me in its naked totality; I felt myself to be transported beyond space and time and literally fed with light.

In my introduction to *Gravity and Grace*, I have described under what circumstances Simone Weil entrusted her notebooks to me on the following day, and the spirit in which she did so.

From Oran she wrote me a long letter: with a presentiment that we should not see each other again, she tore away a little of the veil of reserve and silence which enveloped her friendship: 'It is not surprising that separations should be accompanied by suffering. In all that is painful there is an irreducible core of suffering which is of the same nature as physical suffering. It is undesirable, at least for me, not to feel it, because that takes their reality from sorrowful things. It is desirable only that no more than this irreducible core should be felt, and that it should be allowed to penetrate only into the part of the soul which is made for that, whilst the part which is made for contemplation continues to love and bless God because of his great glory. . . . The same order of the world makes possible meetings and separations. God has given us the joy of meetings and the sorrow of separations. We should welcome these gifts, like all the others, with our whole soul, and experience to the full, and with the same gratitude, all the sweetness or bitterness as the case may be. Meeting and separation are two forms of friendship and contain the same good, in the one case through pleasure and in the other through sorrow. . . . Soon there will be distance between us. Let us love this distance which is wholly woven of friendship, for those who do not love each other are not separated . . . Meeting and separation are the human symbols of the absolute union between the Father and the Son in the Trinity, and of the inconceivable wrenching apart of the Father and the Son at the moment of the words "My God, my God, why hast thou forsaken me?" That is why, for us men, separation is more suitable; for we have the felicity of having been thrown by our birth at the foot of the Cross. . . . You have been, you are and you always will be very much to me. There is nothing I admire so much in you as your friendship for me. These words look like excessive pride, but you know me well enough to see in them an exactly opposite meaning. My gratitude is in proportion. . . . '

I wrote once more to Simone Weil in America. My letter was lucky enough to reach her. She replied to me on 10th September 1942: her message – the last I received from her – is full of regret and remorse at having left her country and her friends in affliction and at not having yet found the way which was to bring her to the confines of self-effacement and sacrifice: ' . . . Your letter is the first that I have received from France. I thought that I was completely forgotten over there, and that seemed perfectly natural. Thank you for your thought of me. . . . Your letter has aroused very painful echoes in me. In my case there are far more serious reasons for being torn, because for me the separation is from a whole country and a country which contains nearly everything I love. And, above all, I am myself the cause of this separation. . . . Thus the pain of separation is made intolerable, sharp and bitter by the sense of my fault. I feel that in leaving my country and my friends in their affliction I am a deserter. . . . One should be able to welcome sorrows and joys with exactly the same gratitude; but it is not possible when the sorrow is mixed with remorse. . . . Actually, the mere thought of the streets of Marseilles or of my little house by the Rhône pierces my heart. . . . '

A few months later she left for England. She was to die there in August 1943, as a result of the privations which wore her out on earth and of that thirst for pure goodness which drew her towards heaven. Do the dead know what they kill in us when they leave us? For us who loved her, a part of our soul has become a tomb: a thousand exchanges which were only possible with her have been swept out of existence for ever. But did she not tell us that truth is on the side of death? We do not have to dwell on her memory: the essential in what she has left us is not a recollection but a reflection of the eternal Presence – and time cannot measure what is not born of it.

Note

[1]   This God who decreed measure and number,
    And instituted unalterable order throughout the universe,
    Behold him under the weight of his creation. . . .
    He has born the outrage of the flesh and the days,
    He knows the torments of exiled love
    Which struggles, quivering in the wine-press of time.
    The One and the ephemeral are joined in him. . . .
        Unpublished poem by G. Thibon. [Translator's note.]

VERTIGO OF THE
ABSOLUTE

Is what we know of the character and interior life of Simone Weil enough to explain her thought, and to account for this unique work of hers which stands out sheer and solitary, like an isolated peak in the immense range of the highest achievements of human genius?

In all work of genius it is important to distinguish between the product of creative skill, invention, etc., and the record of personal experience. Some authors are almost entirely craftsmen and some almost entirely witnesses. The study of *Phèdre* or of the *Légende des Siècles* throws but little light on the personality and interior life of their authors; there is nothing to suggest that Racine or Victor Hugo experienced the sentiments they express; it may well be that their work bears as little resemblance to their souls as a house to the architect who designed it; moreover the materials for such work come largely from outside – from the beauty of the world, tradition, history or the moral or religious atmosphere of the period. But if, on the other hand, we read Pascal or Nietzsche, we feel at once that the author is speaking primarily of himself, that he is fully committed to all he is writing and that it is from his own experience – from an anguish and hope that belong to him alone – that he evolves not only the form but most of the material for his work. The face of Racine himself is very vaguely discernible behind *Phèdre* or *Athalie*, whilst the *Pensées* are like an exact cast of Pascal's features.

Simone Weil belongs unquestionably to the category of witnesses. Her work and her personality throw light upon each other.

Nothing was more foreign to her than the notion of an act or thought detached from man. She did not write one line which was not the exactest possible expression of an irresistible inspiration and, at the same time, an invitation and an engagement to remain faithful to this inspiration, to embody in her whole life and to the very depths of her being what her spirit had glimpsed. The perfect bareness of her style, which reflects her inner stripping, is evidence of the close relationship between her words and her life: the tremendous effort of attention and the atmosphere of prayer, which in her case always accompanied literary creation, tended towards the *verbium vitae* as the curve follows the asymptote.

But the asymptote is for ever inaccessible to the curve which follows it, and no genius is a pure witness except God, whose word wholly exhausts his essence. It is very difficult with someone in whom elements of true sanctity are found in conjunction with a genius for expression – and Simone Weil is an outstanding example of this – to determine what is attributable to sanctity as such and what to genius applied to the study of sanctity. There are outwardly insignificant people who live more than they express, there are others who express more than they live. Every genius is by nature a messenger, and his message has a meaning and implication which reach far beyond himself: there are, as Claudel says, 'Those words within him which are addressed to others.' In speaking of the 'sanctity' of Simone Weil it must always be remembered that he who is inspired always gives more than he has. We are reminded of the admirable words in which Bossuet, replying to Marshal de Bellefonds' expression of gratitude, described the fearful indigence of the man of genius who transmits divine gifts without possessing them: 'Pray for me, poor channel through whom the waters of heaven flow, and who have difficulty in retaining a few drops.'

Simone Weil experienced to the point of torture this disproportion between her message and herself. That is no doubt the secret of the contrast which struck all her friends – the contrast between a pathetic and sometimes excessive humility with regard to herself and an uncompromising assurance, a grim obstinacy (for which she was often accused of pride) with regard to everything concerning her inspiration.

Simone Weil had the greatest contempt for herself as an empirical personality – a 'phenomenal self' to use the language of Kant: her humility in this realm bordered on an inferiority complex. It is enough to make one smile in anyone of her stature, but she was sincerely convinced that she was absolutely lacking in natural gifts on all levels: how many times she spoke to me with dazzled admiration of her brother's genius which served to accentuate her own nothingness! 'One should not dare to form such ideas', she wrote to me one day after having described her literary ideal, 'when one is not capable of work which corresponds to them; it is unfortunate for me that such work should be beyond my powers, and still more unfortunate that I should be equally incapable in every domain.' This humility came on the one hand from an almost constant sense of awkwardness and inhibition – due in great part to ill-health – which made it difficult for her to carry out the humblest tasks, and on the other hand to the very greatness and purity of her inspiration, which by contrast showed up all the weaknesses of her nature. As for this inspiration, she not only felt it to be gratuitous and undeserved, but she was prepared to attribute it to some inconceivable mistake of divine mercy. Every time that I told her of my admiration and gratitude for all that she had brought me, the invariable reply could be resumed as follows: 'You are labouring under a misunderstanding; it is not I; you are taking me for someone else!' I will only quote a few examples chosen at random: 'I own that I am very much touched by what you say to me . . . for I never supposed that anything issuing from me could be beneficial to a human being. I think that, where you are concerned, prejudice in my favour has a great deal to do with it. You must surely have such a prejudice; otherwise why should you think well of me?' And a few months later: 'The first impression I had from your letter was that there must be some mistake or misunderstanding, otherwise such words could not be addressed to me. My second thought was that I must lie a great deal without knowing it for such a mistake to be possible. My third thought was one of very real and deep gratitude because, in spite of everything, such words seem to infuse additional life. But who knows whether that really does good or harm? What is assuredly authentic and true and causes me joy, is that God continues to send you his gifts. The illusion that I have some part in a thing where I can have none is of no importance.' Her last letter marks an advance: she at last accepts the idea that God can make use of her, but only to depreciate the instrument immediately afterwards to the advantage of him who uses it: 'It may be that God has made use of me to draw you a little nearer. He is not hard to please in his choice of tools. He makes a practice of the recovery of refuse. . . . '

The same supernatural inspiration made her see through and trace back to their miserable origin all the states of soul by which a sick and worn-out nature imitates on a far inferior and all too human plane the operations of grace. Here, for instance is what she says of her detachment: 'All sorrow, especially if it concerns me personally, is as it were enveloped on all sides with a layer of indifference. Unfortunately this is not detachment. It is an exhaustion of the sensibility due to an accumulation of sufferings, no doubt not great in themselves but disproportionate to the vital energy. This indifference is an imitation of detachment and results from a biological process, it is like the loss of feeling in a tooth when the nerve is killed and it has no value.' And, in the same letter, at the same time as she rejects my praise, she defines her 'humility' thus: 'There is in me something stronger than the illusions of pride, something which prevents me from believing words of such a kind or even remembering them. Unfortunately this something is not humility. It is a mechanical and worthless equivalent of humility, analogous to the mechanical equivalent of detachment of which I was telling you, and due to the same cause. . . . '

To be quite candid, I must own that such humility, however real and moving it may be, seems to me to be still far enough removed from supreme detachment. Simone Weil's *ego* was not dead: it was engaged in the process of committing suicide in a heroic tension which accentuated its forms and limitations. Saint Thomas tells us that the proud man sins through an 'inordinate appetite for his own excellence'. Might we not suspect Simone Weil of an *inordinate* appetite for her own abasement, in which it is possible to trace a pride revolting against itself? Perfect humility, such as Simone Weil herself describes, is in a sense *impersonal*; it does not have to do with the wretchedness of an isolated individual but with the wretched estate of the creature as such – the nothingness common to all finite beings: 'Do not judge; all faults are equal; there is only one fault: not to have the capacity for feeding on light.' To be distinguished for evil and nothingness, to select oneself for contempt, is still to put oneself forward, it is still a form of pride. In so far as she despises herself Simone Weil forgets to forget herself. Her humility is still partly inspired by a *negative* preoccupation with self: she carves her ego by hollowing it out as the proud carve theirs in relief. The ideal would be to make of it a perfectly smooth surface on which one could glide without stopping. . . .

It was only very rarely that Simone Weil extended her humility, which she drew precisely from her inspiration ('the knowledge of our wretchedness is the only thing in us which is not wretched'), to that inspiration itself. She was quite ready to recognize that ideas came to her by mistake ('I am not a person with whom it is advisable to link one's fate. Human beings have always more or less sensed this; but, I do not know for what mysterious reason, ideas seem to have less discernment'), it was not so easy to get her to admit that these ideas might themselves be mistaken. Her contempt for the inn increased her admiration for the marvellous guest who deigned to shelter in it, and vice versa. How could one blame her; the inn was herself, and the guest came from outside! I know from experience how fiercely she defended her slightest ideas: yet it was not she herself who was in question; for she endured the most violent contradictions without taking the slightest offence; she was simply faithful to the light which had penetrated her soul with irresistible evidence. Mediocre men, who have never been dazzled by a personal revelation and whose entire intellectual baggage consists of a collection of ready-made and interchangeable opinions, are quite prepared to attribute to pride or obstinacy this fidelity to evidence and this courage in faith which uplift the souls of great men. They are very far from guessing that the man of genius sees what others do not see. Even when one is surrounded with blind people (and this is generally the case in spiritual matters, where blindness is the rule and clear vision the exception), there is no presumption in saying: 'I see.' He who at high noon persists in asserting that it is broad daylight is not proud on that account: he is only bearing witness to the light which dazzles him.

For Simone Weil, the problem was a little more subtle. There are two very different elements in all works of genius: the light itself, which depends upon inspiration, and the way in which this light is refracted, coloured and redistributed, which depends upon the personality and limitations of the individual. There is the intuition of genius which is born of a gratuitous and secret contact with unrevealable truth and beauty, and there are the clear and distinct thoughts which interpret it, the words which express it and above all the systems into which we try to fit it. Stanislas Fumet writes somewhere that the mystic can affirm with certainty that he *has seen* and that the danger of error starts when he wants to say precisely *what he has seen*: the same could be said of men of genius. Discrimination is almost impossible in the concrete, especially for the genius himself, so that, powerless to disentangle what is objective in his inspiration from what is subjective, he always runs the risk of slipping unconsciously from fidelity to evidence into pride of spirit. I think it is difficult to avoid the suspicion that such a slipping should have affected Simone Weil: her attachment, not only to the great central intuitions of her genius, but to an infinite number of arbitrarily chosen details, to a thousand eminently subjective interpretations or reconstructions which have more in common with imaginative work or poetic creation than with philosophic or religious contemplation, is enough to convince us of it. Let us be indulgent, however: the man of genius experiences such ecstasy at the unfolding of his creative faculties, the things he discovers appear to him in a light so brilliant and so pure, that a truly superhuman effort of withdrawal and detachment is required of him to discriminate, in his own inspiration, between the part played by God, the ever true inspirer, and that played by the inspired creature, ever prone to err. Nothing is more rare and precious than the humility of genius as *genius*. There is need here for the sharp blade of that interior sword which, according to Saint Paul, separates soul and spirit.

We must hasten to add that Simone Weil had flashes of this supreme humility. The failure of her sanctity to find visible expression and the difficulty she experienced in practising the natural virtues caused her to have bitter doubts about the authenticity of the revelations of her genius. 'Perhaps it is worth no more than the weight of the paper,' she wrote to me one day with reference to her written work. And we found in her American notebooks, by way of conclusion to a long meditation on the mysteries of the faith, this almost despairing confession: 'All these mystical phenomena are absolutely beyond me. I know nothing about them. They are reserved for people who have the elementary moral virtues to start with. I speak about them at random. And I am not even capable of telling myself sincerely that I am speaking about them at random.'

It is by such confessions that we have to judge Simone Weil: they make up for all the exaggerations, narrowness, rigidity or arbitrary systematization there may be in her work. It is in those moments when she is absent from her genius that she appears most truly as a genius: her personal limitations and trials no longer discolour her message; she finally becomes what she has always longed to be: a nothingness which conveys the infinite. . . .

All work of genius reveals something of God through the inspiration it contains. But there is always a risk that it may veil the infinitude of God through its human and limited elements. Eternal truth does not allow of exclusive concessions.

Simone Weil never wanted to monopolize this truth. Those who see her as an infallible guide will gain much by meditating upon the cries of humility which we have just quoted. And those who, hypnotized by what remained in her of intellectual pride, are tempted to reject the whole of her evidence, will perhaps recognize that such flashes of total humility would be impossible in anyone who lived exclusively on ideas, words and falsehood. For us, there is no question of accepting or rejecting the whole of Simone Weil's thought *en bloc*. We receive it with the sovereign liberty of love, which creatures receive from God and which they should exercise in their relations with each other if they are to avoid both indifference and idolatry: 'You have *only one master*, and you are all brothers.' If it is written 'Love one another', it is also written, 'Keep yourselves from idols.'

* * *

Simone Weil suffers from the equivocal situation of those whose genius is of a philosophic and religious order. From the philosophic point of view it is required that their work should be a faithful tracing of objective truth, and from the religious it must be the pure reflection of inner experience. If they depart from these requirements in the slightest degree, they are immediately accused of irresponsibility or dishonesty. Yet no genius is a mere witness: he is not content to discover, he invents; his productions are an amalgam of revelation and creation. Everybody admits this in the case of poets. Why not in the case of philosophers? Are they not to have the same right as others to exercise their creative faculties? Moreover, did the greatest of them ever fail to use these rights? Was not Plato, for example, almost as much of a poet as Homer? Since there are poetic myths, I do not see why there should not be philosophic myths. If that is granted, we can save a great number of things which the bare criterion of fact and fiction would eliminate for ever from the works of the greatest thinkers, and particularly from those of Simone Weil with her unfailing gift for creating myths. Instead of taking what she says literally and accepting or rejecting it according to whether or not it fits in with logic or facts, we should find the true meaning of the construction of her genius and restore to it its deep value which is above all a *symbolic* and *evocative* value. Reality has many levels and perspectives; the *Divine Comedy* and *Don Quixote* are untrue in the order of facts and true in the order of greatness and beauty. Perhaps we should use analogous criteria in order to appreciate the 'mythical' side of the work of Simone Weil. . . .

I have entitled this chapter 'Vertigo of the Absolute'. These words seem to me to sum up the greatness and weakness of Simone Weil's doctrine. Vertigo is caused by the attraction of an abyss and, when this abyss is another name for God, it is good to experience such an attraction. That is where the greatness of Simone Weil lies. But the first effect of vertigo is loss of balance: Simone Weil, dazed by the absolute, staggers and has difficulty in finding her way in the relative. And that is where her weakness lies.

Like all souls marked by God, Simone Weil thirsts for absolute truth and absolute love. Such thirst can find nothing to quench it here below. Everything is compounded of truth and error, of good and evil, everything is born of chance and destined to die,

everything is subject to conditions and limitations. Illusion alone
– the antidote of despair and a cure worse than the disease – can
mask this terrible reality from us. When a man says to a woman:
'I love you', she instinctively receives this avowal of love as the
sign of a unique and necessary choice and of an unconditional
offering. But this love is not necessary: it is born from the chance
of a meeting. Nor is it unconditional: it depends in its every part
upon contingent and transitory dispositions. The woman thinks
she is loved for herself. But what is the self except a tissue of
ephemeral appearances? If the lover owned to her, 'I love you for
your beauty, or your intelligence: my love will therefore last as long
as this beauty or this intelligence, or as long as I continue to need
these qualities in the form in which they exist in you', she would
feel herself penetrated with the coldness of death. Yet that is the
truth of human love, and such truth is made of falsehood. 'It is
untrue to say that love is stronger than death: death is the stronger.'
Simone Weil used to meditate endlessly on a line of the *Iliad*
concerning the dead warriors who had been left unburied: 'But they
lay on the ground, dearer to the vultures than to their wives.' We
love in the same way as we eat – and when we no longer find
anything to feed on in a person, we leave him to those who can still
find something there to devour: the voracious 'love' of the vultures
succeeds the worn-out love of the wives. . . .

Here Simone Weil's reasoning comes strangely near to that of
Pascal: 'What is the self? . . . Does the man who loves a woman
because of her beauty really love her? No, because small-pox which
destroyed the beauty without killing the woman would make him
stop loving her. And if I am loved for my judgment or my memory,
is it really *I* who am loved? No, for I can lose these qualities without
losing my self. Where then is this self, if it is found neither in
the body nor the soul? And how can one love the body or the soul
except for those qualities which do not constitute the self, since
they are perishable? . . . So we never love anyone, we only love
qualities. Let us therefore stop laughing at those people who
claim to be honoured on account of their functions or office,
because we do not love anybody except for borrowed qualities.'
Simone Weil in her turn makes the terrible discovery of relativity
and nothingness which leads either to sanctity or despair according

to whether or not we are able to dominate it in order to go to God. *Everything here on earth is only appearance, and there is no hierarchy in appearances.* 'What does all that amount to – that which is only appearances?' says the poet; the exact echo of Saint Augustine: *quod aeternum non est, nihil est.*

If that which we call being is only an appearance, that which we call goodness has no greater reality. This pitiless lucidity which reduces all created things to chance and illusion cuts away the very foundations of all the customs, all the laws, all the moral codes of our earthly life, for they exist precisely to establish a hierarchy and to mark oppositions among the appearances, to choose some rather than others. For Simone Weil, as for Pascal, La Rochefoucauld or Nietzsche, the virtues and vices cancel each other out and morality is nothing but an ever precarious compromise between incurable egoisms, a mere rule of the game, bringing a little order into the dance of phantoms: 'Admirable rules for preserving order, morality and justice have been drawn from concupiscence' (Pascal). But egoism (Simone Weil would call it gravity), even when it is embanked and codified, does not change its nature, and phantoms, even if they dance without bumping into each other, are no more real for all that. In other words, good and evil, seen as human phenomena of the social order, are only apparently opposed to each other; in reality they are cut from the same cloth; they flow from the same restricted and impure source. 'Good as the opposite of evil is, in a sense, equivalent to it, as is the way with all contraries,' Simone Weil wrote, ' . . . that which is the direct opposite of an evil never belongs to the order of higher good. It is often scarcely any higher than evil! Examples: theft and the bourgeois respect for property, adultery and the "respectable woman"; the savings-bank and waste; lying and "sincerity"' (*Gravity and Grace*, 'Evil').

That force which controls all natural phenomena – psychological phenomena included – and which Pascal calls egoism, La Rochefoucauld self-esteem, and Nietzsche the will to power, is what Simone Weil names gravity. In human relations there is attraction or repulsion, forces are balanced or unbalanced: there is neither truth, nor goodness, nor love: 'All the natural movements of the soul are controlled by laws analogous to those of physical gravity . . . what we expect from others depends on the effect of gravity upon ourselves, what we receive from them depends upon the effect of gravity upon them. Sometimes (by chance) the two coincide, often they do not.' But in order to find the strength to live in an unreal world, we veil this truth from ourselves and we give these mechanical relationships a moral interpretation. When, for instance, someone needs us for as long as we need him, we say he is 'faithful'. But if he continues to need us when we no longer need him we have no hesitation in describing him as a 'hanger-on'. Yet he is the same man, and nothing but the chance which controls our meetings determines our reactions. . . .

Where, then, dwells that unmixed and limitless good to which every soul aspires – that good which an invincible illusion makes us seek in the wrong place? It is outside this world – it is in God. 'The only good which is not subject to chance is that which is outside the world.' In order to find it, it is necessary to realize the nothingness of all created things and to offer God a naked despair. 'We want everything which has a value to be eternal. Now everything which has a value is the product of a meeting and ceases when those things which met are separated. That is the central idea of Buddhism. . . . It leads straight to God' (*Gravity and Grace*, 'Chance'). Here again Pascal has preceded Simone Weil: 'It is good to be weary and tired by fruitless searching for the true good in order to stretch out one's arms to the deliverer . . . I feel that I could have not existed . . . I am neither eternal nor infinite, but I am sure that there is an eternal and infinite being in the world.'

Grace *alone* can halt gravity. We must choose. We can only touch absolute good by renouncing all the phantoms of the cave. 'To detach our desire from all good things and to wait. Experience proves that this waiting is satisfied. It is then we touch the absolute good.' This detachment has to be total: 'Should only a thread remain, there would still be attachment.' All faults are equal and are summed up in a single one which contains them all potentially: the refusal of the absolute void, the need for idols to fill up this void. Here we have Saint John of the Cross's teaching of the All and the Nothing: no matter whether the bird is fastened to the ground by a heavy chain or by the finest thread, it does not fly. . . .

* * *

It is impossible to know what such expressions corresponded to in the soul of Simone Weil. Did she intend to express a meta-physical truth or was she simply speaking as a mystic who, eager to raise herself up to God, saw all the realities of this world as no more than nondescript ballast and a dead weight? The question is all the more difficult to solve since it is possible throughout her work to find a considerable number of passages in favour of either of the two hypotheses.

We do, however, observe in her, though to be sure there is no formal declaration, a fairly pronounced inclination in favour of philosophic and religious dualism. Dualism is the reef on which the navigators who are in too great a hurry to reach the absolute are likely to run aground. There is something Manichean in the spirituality of Simone Weil and her unquestioning admiration for the Catharists was doubtless the result of an inner tendency. At the same time as she exalts God, she depreciates his handiwork: there is still a yawning chasm between the Creator and the creature. On the one side there is a God who is pure goodness and on the other a world which is governed *on all levels* by a Spinozistic necessity. There is no middle term: everything which does not depend directly upon divine love – from the fall of a stone to the vows of lovers – is subject to gravity. This intransigent dualism greatly simplifies the problems; destiny's field of operations becomes a draught-board where only two colours are opposed; the separation of the sheep and the goats takes place here and now. It is an untenable position, all the same, and, like all excesses, inevitably leads to its opposite: Simone Weil herself does not escape from the fatal consequence of all dualism: having always wanted to separate nature from grace, God from the creature, she ends by confusing them. The mechanism of this change-over is very simple; if, in fact, one supposes that the operations of all natural phenomena are controlled by the laws of a blind, opaque and stifling determinism, one is led to attribute a supernatural origin to every gleam of beauty or purity and to every ray of hope of which one can catch a glimpse in this world: if everything which checks gravity comes solely from grace, that is to say from the intimate and supernatural presence of God, the centre and source of all perfection, we are naturally led to suppose that there is some reflection of this absolute perfection in the individuals or peoples in whom we discover the least resistance to gravity or the slightest vestige of authentic good. And conversely, wherever we observe the triumph of gravity, we shall be tempted to reject everything *en bloc* as evil and nothingness. This may perhaps explain the sharp opposition which Simone Weil establishes between force and purity, false and true greatness, etc., and also her unqualified pronouncements for or against this or that person or period of history. The stakes have been deposited and the result is already settled on this earth: the Egyptians, the Greeks, the Gauls and the Albigenses are nearly all on the side of the light, while the Romans and the Jews are on the side of gravity. Simone Weil here comes very near the totalitarianism which she had always opposed so nobly – and this slip is the logical result of her impatience for the absolute.

This arbitrary attribution of the highest natural phenomena to grace reaches its supreme point in the conception Simone Weil has of literary or artistic genius. She starts by affirming that the inspiration of genius can have no source but supernatural revelation. In God, however, the beautiful and the good make but one: grace generates sanctity at the same time as beauty. Conclusion: authentic genius only belongs to saints or, at the very least, to people who aspire to sanctity with all their souls. And if history seems to teach us the contrary, it is because we confuse talent with genius and false greatness with true: 'It is true that talent has no connection with morality; but it is because there is no greatness in talent. It is untrue that there is no connection between perfect beauty, perfect truth and perfect justice; there is more than a connection, there is a mysterious unity, for the good is one. . . . There is a point of greatness where the creative genius for beauty, the creative genius for truth, heroism and sanctity are indistinguishable. We already see in work which approaches this point how the different great qualities tend to become merged – we cannot separate Giotto's artistic genius from his Franciscan spirit . . . nor, when Velazquez shows kings and beggars on his canvas, can we separate his artistic genius from that burning impartial love which pierces to the depth of men's souls. The *Iliad* and the tragedies of Sophocles and Aeschylus bear marks which are a clear proof that the poets who wrote thus were in a state of saintliness. Racine wrote the only work in the whole of French literature (*Phèdre*) which can be placed beside the great Greek masterpieces, and he wrote it at the time when his soul was worked upon by conversion. . . . A tragedy like *King Lear* is the direct fruit of the pure spirit of love . . . Monteverdi, Bach, Mozart were pure in their lives as in their work. . . . ' In French poetry Simone Weil recognizes a current of supernatural purity in the work of Villon ('the greatest of all: we know nothing of his faults, nor even if there was any fault on his part'), and in that of Scève, d'Aubigny, Théophile and, lastly, of Mallarmé, who was as much a saint as a poet. Of prose writers, she names Montaigne, Descartes, Retz, Molière and Rousseau. Pascal is not mentioned.

This unbelievable heap of exaggerations and exclusions shows us to what a degree someone prematurely established in the absolute can make free with history. To be sure, Simone Weil is entitled to show her preferences, and the list which she offers us is made up on the whole of truly great names. We will also grant her that every creation of genius requires a very high degree of fervour and purity in the soul of its author, but nothing authorizes us to conclude from this that such purity extends beyond the region of creative inspiration as such and is to be identified, in its origin and its effects, with the purity of the saints. All that we know of the life of Villon, for example, shows him to have been very far from sanctity. 'Legends and calumnies!' Simone Weil would reply, but there is nothing to prove it. As for Racine, where does she find the mark of sanctity in a conversion which made the author of *Andromaque* into the bigoted and prudent bourgeois who dissuaded his son from marrying Mlle X because her dowry was no more than thirty thousand pounds and her parents seemed likely to live a long time, into the 'king's historiographer', and into the scheming courtier who, with an exquisite sense of the hierarchy of values, wrote to Mme de Maintenon at the conclusion of a profession of religious faith, that he would always have the consolation of having been faithful 'to the king and to the Gospel'? Why does Simone Weil grant to Racine, flatterer of Louis XIV, the privilege of authentic greatness while she refuses even the name of poet to Virgil, simply because he flattered Augustus? And how can we be anything but stupefied with amazement at finding Rousseau on a list of great

Frenchmen where Pascal and Bossuet do not appear? It is a clear case of begging the question; Simone Weil takes it for granted that genius and sanctity must go together, and wherever she thinks she has found genius she concludes there is sanctity, without concerning herself with historical facts. Just where an infinite number of shades and distinctions are necessary, she boldly proposes a single alternative: 'Christ said: "every good tree bringeth forth good fruit, and an evil tree bringeth forth evil fruit" – either the work of art is evil fruit, or the inspiration which brings it forth is near to sanctity.'

We need not be surprised at these extravagances. Simone Weil is here caught by the sheer logic of her dualism between Gravity and Grace, much as Descartes when he refused to allow souls to brute animals[1] was being caught by the logic of his dualism between extension and thought. In either case it is the principle which holds fast and the facts which have to give way. Therein lies the whole danger of Simone Weil's metaphysical thought: the very notion of nature as issuing from God and yet distinct from God, and the exact meaning of the relationship between man and his Creator, are threatened. On the one hand she isolates God as absolute transcendence, and on the other, by attributing to grace all that is pure and great in nature, she opens the way to pantheism. According to whether she turns her thoughts towards Gravity or Grace, Simone Weil oscillates between a pessimism which reduces man to nothingness and an optimism which raises him prematurely to divinity.

Simone Weil is unfair to man when she attributes all his natural movements to the laws of gravity. Yet she acknowledges that creation is a mixture of being and nothingness, of good and evil. She admits also that the proportions of this mixture may vary to an infinite extent ('God', she writes, 'has created a world which allows every degree of good and evil'); what does that mean if not that there is in creatures, *as such*, a gradation, a hierarchy which reaches from the confines of the absolute transparency of God to the opaque boundary of nothingness? Why then should she close this immense fan which spreads to heaven by folding it up on the side of nothingness, why reduce all natural phenomena to the lowest common denominator: that of the inexorable necessity which makes bodies fall to the ground and stars revolve in the abyss? The Platonic theory of participation, which affords a beneficial counterweight to the dualistic tendencies of the father of philosophy, places the problem of creation in its true light. It is no doubt permissible to say that created things are reflections and appearances; limited and ephemeral, in one sense, they are nothing when compared with the infinite and the eternal ('I am He who is, thou art she who is not,' Christ said to Saint Catherine of Siena); but, if they are all equal in their nothingness as opposed to the absolute, they are not equal in value when compared to each other: they come nearer or less near to their divine model. Pascal is right to say that we only love those qualities in man which are borrowed ('it is unjust that men should attach themselves to me'). But he is wrong when he places all these 'borrowed qualities' on the same plane of unreality, for they have not all the same value: it is less vain, for instance, to love someone for his body than for his clothes, and for the beauty of his soul than for that of his body. This is the exact method of reasoning of the *Banquet*, where different stages of creation are conceived of as steps for rising to God. . . . Simone Weil is unjust when she says that 'we love as we eat', for, if human love is always limited, that is not a sufficient reason for reducing it to its lowest forms. And it must further be taken into account that such a form of reasoning, which is based on an identification of limitation with nothingness, presents terrible dangers: nothing is more hurtful than to reveal the wretchedness of the relative to those who are not capable of rising to the absolute; only the love known to saints makes it possible to look beyond appearances without sinking into despair. But saints are rare. . . .

On the other hand the optimism of Simone Weil is a feverish anticipation of the unity of eternal life wherever she thinks she detects the presence of grace. The close connection she establishes between artistic genius and sanctity is very significant in this respect. It is quite true that goodness is essentially one, and that all the perfections – beauty, love, truth – have mysterious affinities with each other. But what is true ideally and for God is not so in fact and for man. Simone Weil forgets that mixture is the law of the temporal and pays little heed to human pluralism. Yet has she not written that 'creation is good broken up into pieces and scattered throughout evil'? Moreover experience is there to teach us that, with the exception of a few cases of *complete* sanctity, the presence of some perfection in a human being can quite well coincide with the most disconcerting deficiencies in other directions. Transcendental qualities, united in God, are pulverized in creation like specks of gold scattered at random in a field of sand. . . .

Simone Weil's conception of the universe brings vertigo; man sees himself hanging there, without ladders or bridges, suspended between necessity and good – between the abyss of gravity and the abyss of grace.

And yet! We find after all that the whole of our criticism of the dualism of Simone Weil is to be found in Simone Weil herself. She admits, with us, that creation allows of an infinity of degrees and that good and evil are so closely intermingled that, as the parable of the wheat and tares teaches us, it is often not possible to separate them without destroying both. Thus she refutes herself. If, in fact, 'God is only present in creation under the form of absence', how can man, who is part of this creation, be capable of intercourse with God, and how can grace, which is pure good, be grafted on to a necessity which is radically foreign to goodness? Yet throughout all her work Simone Weil insists on the points where nature and grace meet. She feels the presence of God in the beauty of the world, which she defines admirably as the harmony between necessity and goodness. But how can there be harmony if there is no affinity? She defends the *metaxu*, that is to say the temporal values (home, country, tradition, culture, etc.), in which good triumphs over evil, and which can serve as intermediaries between man and God. But how can there be a hierarchy of temporal values if everything in time is without distinction, subject to gravity? Finally she makes herself the apostle who proclaims the need for roots; she knows no greater crime than to deprive an individual or a people of their past. But what is the good of being rooted in a world made of appearances and empty of God? In order to uproot oneself afterwards and to offer this sacrifice to God? But if the good is illusory, the detachment must be illusory also. One could thus develop *ad infinitum* the inner contradiction which eats into the heart of Simone Weil's work. She has never clearly effected a union between the two aspects of her thought – and her vision of the created world remains irreparably torn between her philosophy of gravity and her insistence on a need for roots.

We think, however, that this union is possible – provided the thought and above all the expressions of Simone Weil are interpreted in association with the psychological activity of which they were born: that of the search for pure good and the mortal struggle against idolatry. Simone Weil wants to go to God. Idols stop her on the way: she sweeps them all aside with one gesture and includes them all in the same reprobation. She is like a traveller who must at all costs reach his destination in as short a time as possible: it makes no difference whether it is a flock of sheep, a flood or a chance meeting with a friend which hinders him, he does not arrange these various realities in order of importance, he only sees in them a hindrance and a cause of delay! There is the same difference between Simone Weil and a purely speculative philosopher as there is between a guide and a geographer. The geographer studies a region objectively; he describes its physical features, evaluates its riches, etc. The guide, on the other hand, leads the way to a given spot by the shortest route. From his point of view, everything which shortens the distance to the goal is good, everything which increases it is bad. Simone Weil is, before all things, a guide on the road leading the soul to God, and many of her phrases gain by being interpreted not as a description of the country she is crossing but as *advice to travellers*. The first advice she gives is not to bring luggage; the slightest weight will burden and paralyse us in the climb towards God. And therein perhaps lies the germ of her metaphysic of gravity. . . .

It is only in such a perspective that so many passages which are absolutely unacceptable on the speculative plane find their true meaning. Let us take as an example one of the most disconcerting statements of Simone Weil: 'The world, in so far as it is completely empty of God, is God himself. Necessity, in so far as it is absolutely other than the good, is the good itself.' Taken literally what does this mean? What is quite empty of God and absolutely other than good is unmixed evil. Now it is this very evil, *as such*, which we are to identify with God: it becomes a sort of 'moment', or pole of divinity; and of a divinity, moreover, which we have defined as the pure good! All this is absurd. If, however, we are not seeking for the expression of an ontological truth but merely for something to help the 'pilgrim of the absolute' on his way, we shall find that the total acceptance of necessity, nothingness and the void, and the expulsion of all those relative goods which are like idols for us (including those bearing a divine label), create in the soul that state of total purification and detachment which makes it capable of receiving the unknown and transcendent God who gives not 'as the world giveth'. Here we have the 'nothingness, door to the all' and the central law of the great mystical tradition.

It is to be regretted that the actual form of Simone Weil's language so often leads to confusion between the ontological and mystical planes. Once this confusion is removed we can accept without reserve the incomparable lights she brings us in our journey towards God. These lights, born of the meeting of intuitive genius and supernatural love, are too secret, too pure, and sometimes too dazzling to be arranged in a system. They are flashes in the depths of mystery and, like all flashes, they must ever remain separate and free in this night whose thick darkness they pierce and accentuate. Pearls are made into necklaces and stones into houses, but there is neither thread nor mortar which can join together flashes of light. And that is why the systematic side of Simone Weil's work seems so weak and flat in comparison with the elemental flashing brilliance of her thought.

In spite of her logical and, if I may say so, controversial dualism which betrays an interior conflict, an intimate choice and not a law of her being, Simone Weil has not misrepresented the nature of the relations between God and creation. She wages a war to the death with idolatry and, in so doing, she re-establishes the value and dignity of the thing idolized; she restores their original freshness and savour to all those fruits which God offers to our love and which poison the breath of our covetousness. 'This world is a shut door. It is a barrier. And, at the same time, it is a passage.' By breaking down the barrier of idolatry, she opens the passage to love: 'Only he who loves God with a supernatural love is able to see means only as means.'

She invites us to go beyond the world. But this is in order that we may the better see and love it in its entirety. And, as she calls us to the absolute, her appeal rings out like a rallying shout of rescue at a time when humanity, wallowing to the point of insanity in the adoration of the relative, feels the nausea of despair rising to its lips. God alone . . . That is the first commandment of the law, and the first requirement of love. But the true God never gives himself alone: he brings in his train man and the universe, for 'the second commandment is like unto the first'. We should never accuse the saints of mutilating man; they alone possess the secret of unity. The relative, with all its riches and its virtues, never gives us the absolute ('If I have not charity, I am nothing . . . ') and it may always hide it from us, but the absolute can always give us back the relative: 'All those things shall be added unto you' – and that which is added is the whole of creation.

We can indeed certify that Simone Weil, after having caught a glimpse of the absolute, sometimes staggered as, still dazzled, she returned to the relative, but we do not blame her on that account. It is easy enough for the inhabitants of the valley to keep their balance; the narrowness of their horizon guarantees the stability of their wisdom. But vertigo is the privilege and the price of altitude. Let us above all beware of the 'view from down below', which only sees spots in the sun and slag on the heights. We must have contemplated for a long time and with the bitter yearning of helpless desire the summits scaled by Simone Weil, before we have the right to notice the few slips she made as she took her way amidst the abysses.

Note

1 Descartes had a theory that all brute animals were glorified machines.

ON THE THRESHOLD
OF THE CHURCH

The same attraction and the same vertigo of the absolute are found in Simone Weil's attitude with regard to the Catholic Church. In what measure and at what inner depths her soul inhabited the house of God is a secret which was hidden even from herself and which is known only to God. But her constant refusal of baptism and the judgments she passed on the Church are sufficient proof that her conscious doctrinal thought was not Catholic. It has been said more than once that she was on the threshold of the Church. That is true. But the very fact that she remained so near without ever coming inside presents us itself a very serious problem. To refuse to enter when one is on the threshold is the sign of a deep interior separation.

We have too much respect for Simone Weil to exercise upon her memory that indiscreet pressure which we always refrained from bringing to bear on her herself. The attitude of those who seek to make converts at all costs, who are more royalist than the King of Heaven and are always ready to anticipate the workings of grace, seems to us as absurd as it is dishonest. We are not required to baptise after death a person who did not want to be baptised when she was alive. The Church itself has nothing to gain by such all too human activities. Simone Weil needed the Church (we know how important meditation on its dogmas, sacraments and liturgy and on the life and work of the saints was in the final evolution of her thought); the Church does not need Simone Weil. . . .

What we would attempt here is not, indeed, to resolve but to throw a little light on the problem of the relations, at once so deep

146

and so strained, between Simone Weil's thought and the Catholic doctrine. We know, since we are ourselves sons of the Church, what the force was which drew Simone Weil towards the City of God. We do not so well understand the interior obstacle which kept her on the threshold until the very end.

The more I try to remember the long conversations we had on this point – and I find in them a constant ebb and flow of thought and feeling of which her books are far from conveying the mobile subtlety – the more complex the whole question appears.

There was first of all an intellectual difficulty. Simone Weil approached the question of conversion in the same exacting and relentless spirit which she brought to all other matters. This born enemy of compromise and approximation wanted to know exactly what she would be committing herself to by entering the Church. She brought into action all the 'geometrical' side of her thought in order to examine the dogmatic definitions and the decisions of the Councils. And if she found one formula which her conscience did not accept, it was enough to put everything in question again. I can still see her examining the articles of the Council of Trent one by one and ending her comments with a final and irrevocable refusal. This intellectual rigidity may seem surprising: it is, however, strictly logical in a philosophical genius wrestling with conversion. A great many Catholics, born in the Church, nourished by its sap and bathed in its atmosphere, have never thought of asking themselves whether they adhere with all their mind to the articles of the Council of Trent. Often they do not even know them. They inhabit the house; they find warmth and shelter there and do not trouble to test the foundations or to explore all the corners. The Church is their mother; it is always possible to deny it, but after all they did not choose it. Simone Weil, on the other hand, came from outside. She had to choose; and God knows with what care she scrutinized not only the divine soul, but the human body and clothing, down to the minutest details of the outermost garment, of the bride of Christ.

This, however, only puts off the problem. Why, at the end of her perfectly legitimate examination, did Simone Weil refuse to accept Catholic dogma as a whole?

In the first place, we believe it was because her examination remained incomplete. We will not dwell on this point, which Father Perrin has already brought out. Simone Weil had not enough time for a fundamental study of Catholic dogma: her information was often fragmentary or second-hand. Other matters were calling for her attention at the same time – and the boundless width of her vision prevented her from grasping everything with equal depth and thoroughness.[1] Moreover, and this was still more important, the very bent of her creative genius inclined her to construct an edifice for herself rather than to contemplate in an absolutely objective manner a building which was already erected.

The central difficulty, however, and the core of resistance which, if we judge from the gradation of Simone Weil's texts, must have gone on hardening up to the time of her death, was a radical distrust of the Church as a social organization and authority. She readily admitted the necessity for a religious magistracy – though she never clearly defined either its structure or orders – which would dispense the sacraments, hand on the tradition, and, without using compulsion, would teach, guide and warn souls on their journey to God. She did not deny that the Catholic Church filled this rôle, but she reproached it for being at the same time a social and totalitarian organism, modelled on imperial Rome, and confiscating for its own advantage the liberty of man and the gifts of God. Her conscience rebelled against a spiritual power which proclaimed that there was no salvation outside the Church and which anathematized those who rejected its authority. How many times did she not tell me that Catholic totalitarianism was, in a sense, infinitely worse than that of men like Hitler or Stalin, since it condemned all refractory spirits to eternal torture whereas the tyranny of the dictators did at least cease at death!

We will pass over her crude unshaded interpretation of the Church's anathemas. Simone Weil never could – or would – fully realize the distinction between the body and the soul of the Church, or, in other words, between the visible and invisible Church.[2] The central ideal of Protestantism, that the Church is not the Kingdom but a simple means of access to the Kingdom, seems to me to represent her position fairly accurately. She reaproached the Catholic Church, considered as a world power, with identifying itself unduly with the Kingdom of Christ 'which is not of this world'. The confusion is flagrant: the Catholic conception of the Kingdom of Heaven is not the social side of the Church, that is to say the company of all those who fit into its visible framework and obey its ordinances in their literal sense, it is the Church of the Communion of Saints and includes all the elect in heaven and on earth, all the souls of good will to whom the angels promised peace. And just as the mortal body is made for the immortal soul, so the Church, in so far as it is a social formation and temporal authority, only has meaning and value as the way leading to the invisible Church which is the Kingdom of God.

The Church visible and engaged in the world – with all the imperfection and decay which this entails – is joined to the Church invisible as the body is joined to the soul, and the road to its objective. The very condition of man necessitates this. We must not confuse the road with its objective; but neither must we separate them.

Simone Weil wants the objective but she refuses to accept the road. She reproaches the Church for the rigidity and narrowness of its social organization (it is always that Roman side which offends her!) and for the inflexibility of its authority. In this we recognize once more that anarchic leaven which was always present in the depth of her soul and which led her to overrate man's knowledge and liberty. Let us begin by stating that, from the very definition of its magistracy, the Church does not compel. If, in fact, its influence has taken forms which at times come near to compulsion, this is partly attributable to an abuse of power by some of its members and partly to the very nature of its teaching office. Men being what they are, is it possible to conceive of an education which does not admit of an element of authority and, in extreme cases, of compulsion? For there are different grades of liberty – varying from the caprices of children to the independence of the Saints. Education is like pruning a vine, where lower shoots often have to be cut back so that above it may spread out and bear its best fruit. One of the essential rôles of the Church is just this, to protect liberty from itself, to provide a means of training and support for the tender plant which always tends to trail on the ground, and thus to enable it to rise heavenwards. The poet's line, 'All begins with a refusal and ends with bounty', is more applicable to the Church than to any other form of authority. Of course mistakes are always possible, and the Church, in so far as it is human and at times all too human, is not exempt from them. But does a correction wrongly administered put the whole purpose and use of education in question? It is interesting to observe that a spirit so tragically 'free' as Nietzsche could recognize – from an exclusively human point of view – the fruitfulness of a certain exterior discipline in the Church: 'The way in which respect for the Bible has been maintained in Europe until the present day, is perhaps the best element of discipline and moral refinement for which Europe is indebted to the Church. Books of such depth and of such supreme importance require an authority which comes from outside in order to last for the thousands of years which are needed for their full understanding' (*Beyond Good and Evil*).

With the exception of air and water, all those things which nourish, protect, or develop man spiritually or materially, ranging from food and clothing to the highest forms of morality and art, come to him through the channel of society. Even the ideal of anarchy rests on a social basis! Religious truth is no exception to this law; we cannot conceive of a saint who never heard about God from men. Hence the necessity for the visible Church, whose temporal organization provides a bridge between God and man. There is indeed a temptation – and this is where the criticism of Simone Weil finds its true objective – to make of this bridge an end and a dwelling place, to allow the outward body of the Church to veil its invisible soul, and to practise 'the Faith' in a proud and aggressive party spirit – a temptation, in short, to allow the temporal to stifle the eternal, and the social the divine. It is a temptation as old as the sin of idolatry, and one to which, either individually or in groups, members of the Church have constantly succumbed. Saint Peter gave the first example of this engulfment in the temporal. Scarcely had he been appointed head of the Church and custodian of the keys of the Kingdom of Heaven before he rejected the announcement of the death and resurrection of the Saviour – that is to say the defeat of the Church in time and its triumph in eternity – and drew upon himself the terrible reply of Christ: 'Go behind me, Satan: thou art a scandal unto me, because thou savourest not the things that are of God, but the things that are of man' (Matt. xvi. 23). The spirit of Saint Peter was still preoccupied with the mirage of a temporal Kingdom of God. This mirage dies hard among Christians; it takes more or less subtle forms, but remains identical in essence, and it will last as long as the old man and his misery.

This problem of the relationship between the social and the divine, with all the dangers and promises it entails, is admirably set forth in a passage which is too little known, from the pen of the Protestant theologian Alexandre Vinet: 'The soul engaged in the life of religion resembles a ship launched on the waves and crossing the ocean in search of a new world. Religious society is this ocean.[3] It carries us like the ocean, that fluid mass on which the ship traces its path at will without stopping anywhere. The ocean carries the ship, but this same ocean can swallow it up, and sometimes it does so. Society swallows us up still more often, but, after all, it carries us, and we cannot arrive without being carried by it, for it is like the ocean which, less fluid than the air and less dense than the earth, gives way just enough, to support us without hampering our journey towards the truth. Our goal is not at the bottom of the abyss, it is beyond the ocean. . . . It is enough to give up the hull of our ship to the element which supports us. It is possible to go down in the ocean of society as in the ocean of our globe, and there is no need to ask ourselves in which of the two shipwreck is more frequent.'

The last sentence makes one tremble. We have only to look within and around us and to examine those poor virtues, degraded into social machinery and eager to be seen of men and to receive their reward here on earth, in order to understand, as clearly as Simone Weil did, how serious is the threat of shipwreck in the social element. And we have only to compare our fanaticisms and intolerances with Saint Paul's immortal passage on charity in order to measure all the distance which separates us from that *universality of love* which the Church expects of us. But, once again, we must remember that this risk of shipwreck is the price of the journey; we cannot avoid running it, and we need the Church, even in its most human form, just as the ship needs the sea. All forms of society (family, country, etc.) can give rise to idolatry; that which is inspired by the Church is certainly the worst of all, for it prostitutes the very attributes of God; it makes something human out of what is divine and deserves the terrible anathemas of Isaiah – anathemas which Christ himself renewed.

Following on from our conversations, I wrote Simon Weil a long letter which the impossibility of all communication prevented me from sending to her. I will quote a few passages from it here, while apologizing for the personal accent:

'Everywhere – even in that society with a divine soul, the Church – I see, as you do, the pharisaism, the conventionality, the false virtues and false glories, all that deception which is inherent in social things and which threatens the divine purity within us. And what moves me most is not that this evil is real and deep, but that it is necessary, that it is the inevitable price that has to be paid for the survival of a sacred tradition, that it is the cement, not only of order and civilization, but of the very house of God, and that, without it, humanity would most certainly sink into chaos and barbarism. This armour of conventions and lies risks stifling the divine germ, and at the same time it protects it. It is no easier to dissociate them than to separate the wheat from the tares before the harvest: *ne forte eradicatis simul et triticum*. In the Church, as elsewhere, good and evil will not be separated until they are separated by God after the harvest in another world. Here on earth they are indissolubly joined to each other. This is a scandal for the weak or for the unintelligent of whom Pascal speaks, but it is a necessity. It comes from the very nature of this transitory world. A life subject to duration and death cannot be conceived of otherwise; *mixture is the law of the temporal*. It is unavoidable that this transitory world, where we have the two-fold duty of accepting life as long as it lasts and consenting to death when it comes, should be compounded of good and evil. For, if it were only evil, how could we consent to live? And if it were only good, how could we resign ourselves to dying? Nothing absolute can exist in what is passing, and that is why, wherever pure good or pure evil are found, there also is eternity. . . .

' . . . It is impossible for man to live materially and spiritually – it is even impossible for him to know and love God – without social deception. All revolt, all anarchy even, leads to a new uniformity – generally worse than that which it has destroyed. (Modern history is eloquent enough with regard to this.) So then it is not a question of pursuing and dreaming of an impossible purity but of recognizing and defending that form of society which is least impure: that form which does not stifle all interior liberty and purity but provides a social covering with pores (like skin has), through which the divine can penetrate right to men's souls. It is here that we can measure the necessity and beneficence of the Church. No doubt, as a human society, it overflows with pharisaism and impurities; it still gives too much to Cæsar – for what it calls God is only too often Cæsar in disguise – but, all the same, it makes it possible to render to God a little of what is God's. Outside the Church, everything goes to Cæsar. . . . '

The Latin word *traditio* means at the same time transmission and treason. It is easy enough to accuse the Church of having betrayed the evangelical revelation. It may have done so by accident, and on points where its essential infallibility is not involved. But – and here we touch the core of contradiction and ingratitude which is found in all *great* detractors of the Church, such as Nietzsche or Simone Weil – it is because of what it transmits that we judge what it betrays: it is in the name of the ideal of evangelical purity which it has never ceased to spread throughout the world that we condemn whatever in the Church does not accord with the Gospel. We see this poor human body of the Church to be so impure because we compare it with the divine soul which inhabits it. But, when we do this, we sin grievously against the whole, we arbitrarily separate what God has joined together. Simone Weil, who had fed her soul on the Gospel, the liturgy, Christian art, Saint Francis of Assisi and Saint John of the Cross, found it easy enough, by contrast, to pour scorn on the social side of the Church. But would this current of supernatural beauty ever have reached her without the external discipline which revolted her? She condemned the bark of the tree, and yet all the time she was slaking her thirst from the sap *transmitted and protected by this bark*. We known only too well that the Church has always had within it a materialistic tendency which seeks superficial expansion and social triumph at the expense of interior purity, and which, in its extreme form, could adopt as a motto: 'Let the soul die so long as the body lives!' But the idealistic tendency, which would be ready to break the human channel in order to liberate the divine stream, and of which the motto is 'Let the body perish so long as the soul lives!' is also dangerous. In the life of individuals as in that of societies (including religious society), there are times of crisis when a great many concessions must be made to the body, if only to safeguard the future of the soul which is bound to this body. I do not remember the name of the gifted humorist who wrote: 'It was not by chance that Christ entrusted the keys of the temporal kingdom to the apostle who could sleep while his Master was in agony and denied him in the hour of danger.' And to be sure, in the Garden of Olives as in the Court of the High Priest, and on the road later, when he was flying from Rome and persecution, Saint Peter showed in a very personal manner his anxiety to take care of the 'body' of the Church. But the same apostle knew also how to bear witness to his Master for thirty years, and finally how to die for him. This tension between soul and body is inherent in the Church's life in the world; it constantly exposes it to the danger of exaggeratedly rigid discipline and political compromise,[4] but to avoid taking undue scandal it is enough to remember that its divine soul is inseparable from its human body.

The temptation to shake off the yoke of the Church by revolting against its social side often attacks souls thirsting for interior life and personal contact with God.[5] We escape from it once and for all when we realize that it comes from the need for absolute purity, which the Church itself has implanted in us and which the Church alone can satisfy in an *enduring and universal* manner. It was to this effect that I wrote to Simone Weil: 'Whatever may be the dark corners, the crumbling walls and the vulgar ornamentation found in it, I cannot and I never shall be able to refuse to see the underlying balance and the unique and total grandeur of this wonderful edifice whose foundations are rooted in millennial ages and whose pinnacle is lost in the heavens. It is there, and there alone, that I have found, joined together as two lovers, order and the absolute which everywhere else oppose and devour each other. Its dogmas, sacraments and liturgy have imprinted upon my soul a mark which nothing will ever be able to efface. If (as I pray to

God may never happen) I were obliged one day to separate myself from the Church, it would be on account of requirements which the Church itself implanted in me. I could strike it with my hand, but all the force of that hand would be derived from the nourishment the Church has poured into me. My revolt would always be less deep than my faith, and it would still be an act of faith. . . . '

Moreover, as to that obedience to the Church as a social power, those less elevated devotions, and virtues encumbered with idolatry with which Simone Weil so greatly reproached Catholicism, do they not represent all the religion granted to certain souls? And may they not be a transition or stage on the way towards the higher levels of faith? The 'impurities' of the body of the Church are explained by the fact, not only that it is made *of* men, but that it is made *for* men. I shall never forget the pithy reply of an old Capuchin monk to a young man who was indignant because the Church encouraged certain devotions which seemed to him of an inferior order: 'Sir, Catholicism is a manger where there is hay at the right height for all muzzles.' I must own that I see in this a supplementary proof of the divinity of the Church rather than a cause of scandal. A religion which meets the need of the devout old woman who goes into the house of God to gain an indulgence as one puts a penny into a slot for a bar of chocolate, and which can at the same time satisfy the highest aspirations of a Pascal – a religion thus adapted to all men – does really bear the stamp of the Creator of the universe. We feel in it the presence of that infinite wisdom which, in the words of this same Pascal, 'goes from one extremity to the other and fills up all that comes in between'. But, by a strange paradox, those who are most ready to accuse the Church of lacking universality are also the first to reproach it with being all things to all men.

Simone Weil, with her vertigo of the absolute, pronounces exclusions where it would be enough to establish a scale of virtues. She throws wide the doors of the temple, but, intoxicated with the height, she does away with the steps, and the religion she proposes to us appears to be a thousand times more rigorous and more loaded with anathemas than the Catholicism whose narrowness she condemns! Instead of levelling the roads leading to God she makes of the narrow way a path too steep for human weakness.

* * *

This question, however, is not the essential one. Simone Weil was not a Catholic and we should not look to her for lessons in orthodoxy. What she brings us is an impetus, a call and also the account of an interior route towards pure good, towards the God whom we so lightly name our God and who, even when we know all that human speech can reveal of him, still remains the unknown God.

Simone Weil offers us 'a fountain of water springing up into life everlasting'. As for the channels through which it is to flow, it is for us to provide them and we shall find them without difficulty in the dogmatic and moral system of the Church. Her work swarms with heresies no doubt, but we have the equipment to rectify them. And besides, do we measure the value and fruitfulness of religious inspiration *solely* in terms of strict orthodoxy? We have to raise the level of our discussion and to stop considering Simone Weil only from the point of view of her relations with Catholicism and her failure to become a convert. We have to consider her rather in the timeless setting where her supreme inspiration belongs. We must rise above our all too present controversies, polemics and passions, and read her as, for example, we read Plato. If we look for 'heresies' in Plato, we shall find them easily enough. It is none the less true that there is more religious vitality and certainly more authentic Christianity in the works of the philosopher who provided the Early Fathers with the conceptual material for their theological edifice than in some pious book where everything is second-hand (or nth hand) and where the 'strict orthodoxy' is no more than hearsay and repetition, expressing the mechanical docility of a mind incapable of rising to the level of religious preoccupation and intellectual curiosity where heresy germinates. . . . Unfortunately there is an 'orthodoxy' which can be identified with conformism, just as there is a 'chastity' which is the result of impotence. It is when we consider this laziness of spirit disguised as faith that we understand the full meaning to Saint Paul's declaration that heresies must needs come. . . .

The great lesson Simone Weil teaches is found in the following aphorism: 'The philosophical cleansing of the Catholic religion has never been done. In order to do it, it would be necessary to be inside *and* outside' (*Gravity and Grace*, 'Intelligence and Grace'). The word philosophical is equivocal: I should prefer psychological or moral. Moreover it is not true to say that this cleansing has never been done: all the Saints, all the great Catholic minds, have been engaged in it. Let us say rather that it always has to be done again, for each generation brings the dust and mud of the century's roads into the temple. It is necessary to be both inside and outside: inside, because only those who belong to the house have the right and the duty to sweep it, and outside – that is to say in God, at the heart of the invisible Church – in order to have the interior light which shows up the impurities. This cleansing began on the day when Christ drove the merchants out of the Temple: so long as our left hand knows too much about what our right hand is doing, so long as pharisaical virtues are eager for a temporal reward (whether in the form of interior consolation, social triumph, pride or vengeance), we are all bargaining with heaven. Simone Weil's whip calls us to order, that is to say it brings us back to a sense of our nothingness and to the unconditional love of God.

To be sure – and it is probable that Simone Weil did not sufficiently realize this – all the mediocre and impure virtues which abound in the Church may be the first rough sketch of divine life. But the unfinished sketch with its immature complacency soon hardens into a caricature. It is this caricature of the Church – a caricature which we all bear within us – that Simone Weil attacks with such force – and such justice. We must, above all, take care that we do not seek in the criticism of her mistakes an excuse for refusing her lessons. Do not let us give way to the loathsome inclination which she describes as follows: 'All that is vile and mediocre in us revolts against purity and, in order to save its own life, seeks to defile that purity.' I should like to be sure that none of the recent criticisms of Simone Weil spring from such a poisoned source. Wounded in our nothingness (the worst wounds are those which expose the interior void . . .), we are easily tempted to make of that Catholic truth which we know so well and live so badly, a shield against all reproaches and good examples coming from outside; and we proceed to attach to this very personal protective measure which insures that we shall sleep comfortably in our mediocrity, the flattering label of faithfulness to the Church.

'When we say: "We Catholics", we have already ceased to be catholic,' writes Gabriel Marcel. And Mgr Journet reminds us very opportunely that the frontier of the invisible Church passes through each of our hearts. Since we belong to the visible Church, let us strive to purify our faith and love so that the two frontiers may coincide within us, and let us avoid condemning others in the name of our membership of the sacred organism which we betray by our pride. That is still the best way of refuting the heresies of Simone Weil; and, at the same time, it is the best homage we can pay to the positive part of her message – a message bidding us rise to those higher regions where there are no more heresies because eternal love is there married to eternal silence.

A bad tree cannot bring forth good fruit. All that we know of Simone Weil – and especially that memory of light and charity which she has left for ever in the souls of those who knew her at all intimately – makes us guess that she belonged to that Church of the Saints, whose life is hid in God. Simone Weil loved the soul of the Church passionately; she fed upon it, she drew from it her highest reasons for living; her only mistake was to forget that this soul trailed after it a body with all its weaknesses and demands. Moreover she did not only live by the Church, but she longed to die for it. In writing to me shortly before her departure for America, she ended a long explanation of her reasons for putting off baptism by saying: 'I should be more ready to die for the Church, if one day before long it should need anyone to die for it, than I should be to enter it. To die does not commit one to anything, if one can say such a thing: it does not contain anything in the nature of a lie.' That depends upon the cause for which one dies: to die for an idol would always contain a lie. If Simone Weil longed to die for the Church it was because she was conscious of the stream of eternal life flowing in her. She refused the partial engagements which require the acceptance of the dogmas and discipline of the Church, but she was ready for the total engagement of death. How heavy with meaning is this avowal on the lips of one who said, – 'Truth is on the side of death', and who found only two perfectly pure instants in human existence – the moment of birth and the moment of the last agony. In offering her death to the Church, Simone Weil was at the same time giving it her true birth. We think that this simple sentence closes the discussion, it places Simone Weil where she belongs: at the height where tongues, prophecies and knowledge fade away, but where that charity which is God remains for ever; it unites that which is eternal in her soul and spirit with that which is eternal in the Church.

Notes

1   Simone Weil has been criticized a great deal for the syncretic spirit which led her to establish more or less rash connections between the myths of ancient religions, poetic fiction, or even fairy stories and the dogmas of Christianity or the theology of the sacraments. It is obvious that such comparisons make for confusion and scepticism. But we can also find in them – provided we do not spread everything out on the same level, as Simone Weil too often did – a powerful confirmation of faith; it is not a small thing to discover in the wisdom, religion and poetry of all time and all peoples, a more or less veiled hint of the same eternal truths which the Christian revelation came to rescue from their matrix of illusion and impurity.

2   The pages that follow form a personal dialogue with Simone Weil rather than an objective lesson in theology and I should like to specify the precise meaning of my vocabulary. By the visible Church, or the body of the Church, I wish to designate not only the dogmatic, sacramental and hierarchical system of Catholicism, but the sum of all the individuals – priests, faithful, saints and sinners – who belong visibly to the society known as the Catholic Church. In this sense the visible Church coincides to some extent with what the Gospel calls the 'world'; that is to say, there are members of the body of the Church who are not quickened by the Holy Spirit – the soul of the Church. When I speak further on of the relations between good and evil within the body of the Church, I do not mean that membership of the visible Church implies the slightest acceptance of evil as such; the mixture of good and evil is here a necessity of fact and not of right: since the Church needs a social framework and that cannot be exempt from sin, we have to put up with this blending of good and evil, while struggling with all our might against the evil. What we love in the more or less constantly sick body of the Church is not the sickness but the body – the support and instrument of the immortal soul. And for the love of this body, we are obliged to put up with the sickness. But to put up with does not mean to approve. Our reflections on the link between the good and evil in the Church have no other meaning.

3   From the Catholic point of view the Church, in so far as it is a human society and a temporal organization, can very well be compared to the ocean.

4   People sometimes become indignant about the political 'cuisine' (cooking) of the Church. But, precisely, there must be a minimum of cooking to feed the

body! It does happen, alas! that this minimum is exceeded: the body could often do with simpler food and the soul would be freer. The Saviour reminded Martha, who was too busy with household tasks and asked her sister to help her, that 'One thing is necessary. . . . '

5 Pascal knew this temptation: 'If my letters are condemned in Rome, that which I condemn in them is condemned in heaven. *Ad tuum tribunal Jesu, appello.*'

Made in the USA
San Bernardino, CA
11 December 2014